Ralph Miller:
Spanning the Game

**Ralph Miller
with
Bud Withers**

Champaign, Illinois
61824-0673

Book design: Brian J. Moore
Cover design and
photo insert layout: Michelle R. Dressen
Copyeditor: Lisa A. Busjahn
Proofreader: Phyllis L. Bannon
Front cover photo: Dan Root
Back cover photo: David Nishitani

10   9   8   7   6   5   4   3   2   1

Library of Congress Catalog Card No.: 90-62970
ISBN: 0-915611-38-4

We have made every effort to trace the ownership of all copyrighted material and to appropriately acknowledge such ownership. In the event of any question arising as to the use of any material, we will be pleased to make the necessary changes in future printings.

Sagamore Publishing, Inc.
P.O. Box 673
Champaign, IL 61824-0673

Printed in the United States of America

I dedicate this book to my wife Jean, who is in every way my partner and right hand, and to our children Susan, Cappy, Paul, and Shannon. They, ever at my side, have shared all of the joy, satisfaction, hardship, frustration, and challenge inherent when one follows a quest.
—R.M.

To Velvet, for understanding.
—B.W.

Contents

Acknowledgments

Writing about my life and livelihood is like looking at myself in the mirror at age 70. Because we are all genetically engineered, I am to a large degree beholden to my parents for much of my physical makeup. The rest of my makeup, warts and all, has been of my own making, with a huge contribution from lady luck. I was born with physical attributes that allowed me to participate in all sports at a time when sports, especially basketball, entered the Golden Era.

Moreover, Chanute, Kansas was only 90 miles from the University of Kansas, where I later played under the dean of basketball coaching, Dr. Forrest "Phog" Allen, and was privileged to know professor James Naismith, the father of basketball. Later pages will detail the evolution of this great game as I have known it. I have many to thank for my achievements.

As a coach, I will always cherish my association with the young men who strove under my sometimes harsh criticism to be the very best they could be. I find great satisfaction in watching their success in other professional and personal endeavors. Many of them are close friends and some are proud grandfathers!

I was also fortunate to be assisted on the bench by a few great men. They and I know that I could not have functioned without their tireless efforts. They fielded the complaints, dusted off the egos, counselled the girlfriends, sold the recruits, and placated the fans. They were damn good coaches. I value their loyalty and friendship to this day.

A coach's public relations is often as good as his secretary, and I have had two of the very best. Their knowledge, understanding, and diplomacy made me look good, and I am deeply grateful to them both.

Good managers and trainers are absolutely essential to the well-being of a team. Their work is never done. I've known trainers to spend nights nursing sprained ankles and other ailments to ready players for the next game. Their unique position—to supervise as well as counsel—is very special. Our successes on the road were often directly related to their efforts.

My thanks to all those in the athletic departments who worked on behalf of basketball, directly and indirectly. My thanks also to the sports information directors, some of whom helped us acquire pictures for this book; to the ticket managers; to game-management personnel; to our great fans; and to all who sacrificed their time and efforts in fund-raising. All these people have provided their own special kind of teamwork. I salute the Shocker Clubs, the "I" Clubs, and the Beaver Clubs, as well as the faculty who have acted as members on athletic boards or on NCAA committees. They have served us well, as have the administrators.

Everyone in this profession knows that you must please the fans. May I say at this point how much the fans have pleased me. I continue to correspond with some fans whom I have not seen for years. Basketball is a game for all ages; and, through the years, I have met thousands of fans. As the game has touched their lives, so have they touched my life.

For the most part, I have thoroughly enjoyed my contacts with the media. They are guys and gals doing a job, and I hope I have educated a few of them along the way about basketball. One of my favorites, who worked for the Eugene, Oregon *Register-Guard* when I first went to Oregon State, was Bud Withers. Although he was in the land of the Ducks, he gave us great coverage and became one of the group who covered our team on the road. Bud, who has been responsible for writing this book, is now with the *Seattle Post-Intelligencer*. He is a consummate professional, and I am deeply grateful for his patience, time, and effort.

My career has been long and meaningful. For those who venture to read about it, I hope you find it worth your while.

—R.M.

*　　　*　　　*　　　*　　　*　　　*

For their valuable and varied efforts, thanks to the following: Skip Myslenski, Bill Plaschke, Mike Corwin, Jeff Martin, Ron Bellamy, Shannon Fears, Katy Khakpour, Cindy Darling, Alan Tanner, Bill Knight, Dan Root, Cynthia Gabel, Gen Withers, George and Kathy Martin, and not least, Jean and Ralph Miller.

—B.W.

Part I
Starting Out

1

From Here to There

There was no time for retrospection, no time to get sentimental.

An NCAA tournament comes with a multitude of surprises and intrigue. As a coach, you wake up one morning and don't know whether your team will make the tournament, or who you'll play, or where. So you learn your fate, scurry around, gather videotapes, get scouting reports, and then you play. And because you're a competitor and you have faith in your system, and your players are capable, you think you're going to win.

Sudden Death

I was in Tucson in March, 1989, eight days after my 70th birthday. I was coaching Oregon State in my 38th season of college basketball. We were a sixth seed in the West Region of the NCAA tournament, paired against Evansville, an 11th seed. Everything was pretty much routine. We were playing the first game of the subregional so that meant an early wake-up. Players ate a pre-game breakfast, got taped, and got on our bus to the McKale Center. As I had done for years, I stole off for a cigarette and some idle conversation. Soon, the teams were tipping it off.

We drew out to an 11-point lead early, directed by Gary Payton, our All-America guard, but soon it was obvious we were in for a struggle. Our post defense was spotty, Evansville put together a 10-2 run, and we were ahead only narrowly, 39-37, at the half.

In the second half, we hit a five-minute cold spell that put us in trouble. We weren't the kind of physical, pounding team that could overcome a streak of poor outside shooting.

Soon we were down the stretch. Evansville strung together 11 straight points and led 73-64 with less than five minutes left, and we faced an eight-point deficit with a little more than two minutes to play. Yet Payton, indomitable as always, hit a layup and a three-point shot to start our comeback, plus another two free throws with 11 seconds left to tie the score and send the game to overtime.

My team had bought me another five minutes in my profession.

As a young man, I had never intended to be sitting at the end of a bench orchestrating a basketball team. After World War II, my wife Jean and I had settled east of Los Angeles in Redlands, California. I was a citrus fruit distributor, thinking I was going to get rich. Coaching the game was the furthest thing from my mind.

I guess I had seen just about everything. I had played for one of the great minds of the game, Dr. Forrest "Phog" Allen, at the University of Kansas. At Kansas I knew Dr. James Naismith, the inventor of the game. I didn't know him well, but I knew him. I coached against Henry Iba, Eddie Hickey, Bob Knight, and Dean Smith.

But there I was, coaching my 1,044th college game. My teams had won 670 college games, good for sixth on the all-time list. Before that, my three years-plus of coaching high school teams had netted 63 victories. Because of these victories, I had been inducted into the Naismith Hall of Fame in Springfield, Massachusetts, a cherished honor that helped me forget the many disappointments in the NCAA tournament.

Before the 1988-1989 season began, I had made my intention to quit coaching known. Whenever the season ended, I was going to toss away the chalk, turn away from the blackboard, and call it quits. My team extended my last season. We went 22-7 and were invited to the NCAA tournament.

Now we were in a dogfight with Evansville. We took a three-point lead in the overtime, but could not maintain it. Evansville was deadly from outside. We had a 90-89 lead, but with ten seconds left, Reed Crafton knocked in a 25-foot shot with Will Brantley all over him, and we trailed 92-90.

With five seconds remaining, Payton, who had carried us so many times, launched a three-point shot from the left wing—missed it, scrambled for the rebound, and fouled out.

The die was cast. Evansville hit a pair of clinching free throws and won, 94-90. I had coached a thousand games, but I was shocked. The NCAA tournament is so furious and so final. I don't think I even considered it might be my last game. We didn't expect to lose.

In the interview room I made a few comments. The press gave me a round of applause as I departed. Then I went back to the hotel, packed, and got on a plane for home. I had begun this foolishness, coaching basketball teams, back at Mt. Oread High School in Kansas in 1941.

Now it was over.

Sports in My Blood

My story begins on March 9, 1919. I was born in Chanute, Kansas, the son of Harold Miller and Ruth Lucille Filson Miller. My father was a history teacher and a good athlete who lettered in basketball at the University of Kansas. He went on to be a coach and administrator.

My mother was a college graduate with teaching credentials and an athlete in her own right. In fact, she was an all-state basketball player for five years in high school, and during her time at Chanute, the school won four state girls championships and was runner-up the other year. So I guess my bent for athletics was sparked from both sides of the family.

My family's roots are deep in Chanute, which is in southeastern Kansas, not far from the borders of Missouri and Oklahoma. Chanute in the early 1900s was a bustling railroad town, the divisional headquarters for the Santa Fe Railroad. The railroad attracted many people to the area. By 1906, there were 10,000 people there, but the town never reached a population of 11,000.

My grandfather, Enoch, became the engineer on the Santa Fe run between Kansas City and Tulsa. There was a roundhouse outside Chanute, and an engineer would make the run from Kansas City to Chanute, and that was the end of his day. Then another engineer would take the train on to Tulsa, and they'd return the next day. A great highlight of my life when I was seven or eight was to ride an engine with my grandfather from the railroad station out to the roundhouse.

One of my earliest sports memories is of playing golf at age six. My grandfather Filson gave me a set of clubs. I played with my parents and I used to tee off with my mother at the women's tees. One day my dad, who had a tight hook, started to hit his second shot out beyond the women's tees. My mother said, "Harold, Ralph hasn't teed off yet."

My dad said, "Ah, it doesn't make any difference. He can't hit the ball this far."

Well, I did hit it that far—squarely on the back of his head. Dad never left the tee again until after my drive.

My teenage years were those of the Great Depression, but I couldn't actually say the Depression bothered me very much. I don't ever remember my parents not having a car. The dust-bowl days of the 1930s, memorialized by John Steinbeck in *The Grapes of Wrath*, did not really reflect life in Chanute. This was partly because Chanute was dependent on the railroads, partly because the severe dust was more prevalent in western Kansas and Oklahoma. Yet, we had dust quite often.

I remember that on occasion there would be so much dust that it looked like dusk at noon; and, if it happened to rain, we had to go out and wash our houses. In fact, I remember that the morning after we won the state basketball championship in 1935, we returned to Chanute with the car lights on because a heavy dust storm had limited visibility.

Chanute had two railroads, and a cement plant. The city also owned the waterworks and electrical plants so it was reasonably well off. Jobs weren't unavailable during the Depression days, and we didn't have a great exit of the townsfolk. I remember my dad's top salary back in those days was $1,800 a year, and that wasn't too bad. We didn't have much money to spend, but I didn't think life was too difficult.

I was exposed to many different things as a boy, not just basketball. I could play the violin and baritone sax. I don't think I had a favorite sport. By the time I left high school, I had participated in football, basketball, track, baseball, softball, swimming, tennis, and, golf in school-sponsored, church-sponsored, and summer-league programs. My father didn't force me into playing, but he made sure the opportunities were available.

My first hero was Jim Thorpe. I knew all about Jim Thorpe, Red Grange, and Babe Ruth. As a very young child, my grandfather had a wireless radio and let me listen to a round or so of one of the great Dempsey-Tunney fights of 1926 and 1927.

My first real taste of basketball came in the fifth or sixth grade. My dad was principal of the high school in Chanute. During the cold winter months, I made a habit of going over to the high school gym, which was only a block from our home. I'd take along a ball and sometimes get to shoot a hoop while the high school team practiced.

Then I discovered that on Tuesdays and Thursdays, the girls' intramural basketball program had the court from 4:00 to 6:00 p.m. Fortunately for me, they were always short of personnel so I became a substitute for the high school girls team. I was tall for my age; I reached 6' 2" at age 13 and never grew any more. That was the first time I remember playing in a gymnasium. I admit I was a little selfish. I kept it a secret so nobody else from the fifth and sixth grades got to play except me.

Because we had a car, I had opportunities to see football games at the University of Kansas. The first time my dad took me to a game in Lawrence ended up being one of the most embarrassing moments of my life. We had a Model-T Ford. There was a steep hill on 14th Street and my dad had used so much gas driving the 90 miles from Chanute that the car wouldn't go up the hill because the carburetor was a gravity-flow type. So he backed all the way up the hill to use the gravity. Today I realize that wasn't anything unusual, but on the occasion of my first visit to Lawrence, and my first football game, I felt sure that everyone was watching us.

I mentioned my mother's success playing basketball shortly after the turn of the century. It probably seems incongruous today because the rise of women in athletics really began with Title IX, the federal legislation of the early 1970s.

Well, oddly enough, it wasn't unusual for women in my mother's day to have the outlet of athletics. When Dr. Naismith invented the game of basketball back in 1891, he invented it for men and women. So until the 1920s, girls had competitive basketball. Then it was decided girls shouldn't be competing like that.

Instead they should be young ladies and work on their posture and other foolishness. From that time on, the only three states that stayed with girls basketball were Iowa, Texas, and Oklahoma. Until the 1920s, girls competed in basketball in a majority of the United States.

When I was inducted into the Naismith Hall of Fame at Springfield, Massachusetts a few years ago, my sister was with me. There was a picture hanging there of my mother's high school Kansas state championship team in 1911, but nobody knew who it was. The picture was rather funny, the girls were lying flat with their chins resting on their hands. I think five were on the bottom and two were on the top, all stretched out. My sister spotted the photograph, and as a result, they were able to identify the girls in the picture.

The cutoff for women's basketball was roughly 1920. This was unfortunate for women participating in sports until the 1970s. In fact, my daughters are a graphic example of the time frame. My youngest daughter, Shannon, was in junior high school when Title IX came into effect so she was able to participate. Later she became the only woman in the history of Oregon State to win three letters in a single year. My older daughter, Susan, might have been a good athlete, but she never had the chance to prove it. The opportunity simply wasn't there.

I guess I had sports in my genes. The only sports I played that I didn't like were baseball and boxing. The action was a little too slow for my tastes in baseball, and I didn't enjoy getting hit in boxing. On the other hand, I really liked track. My dad had acquired a high-jump apparatus, and by putting boxes under the standards, I could raise the bar to eight feet. I had a long running path and a dirt pit in my backyard, and I could pole vault eight feet by the time I left grade school.

On one occasion in a junior high school dual meet, the coaches allowed us to enter as many events as we wanted. I decided to enter all of them, and won every event except the broad jump, where somebody defeated me by a quarter of an inch.

We were fortunate to have a solid group of athletes during my high school days at Chanute. In a four-year period, we managed to win all but four of our basketball games and all but three football games. We won the state championship in basketball in 1935 and took second place in 1937. I was named to all-state teams in both sports for three straight years, playing forward and quarterback. Those were the days when blacks participated separately. They had their own state championships and the black team of Chanute also won the state title in 1935.

My indoctrination to thinking like a coach was in ninth grade. I went in to see our football coach, Dale Skelton. He was a huge, lean man, 6' 7", and about 260 pounds. He had been a fine football player and track man. He said to me, "I understand you'd like to be a quarterback."

I said, "Yes, sir."

"You know," he said, "in football, you've got 11 people, and during the game, one of them sometimes forgets an assignment. So there has to be one player on the field who knows the assignment for every player for every play we have. Do you know who that would be?"

I said, "No, but I am getting the drift. I believe you're talking about the quarterback's responsibility."

"Yes, I am," he said. "Here's your playbook."

It consisted of 125 plays out of five formations. I learned them all. So I thoroughly understood the game of football at age 14. Of course, the same concepts applied to basketball. So I've understood offense and defense ever since I started to play the games: Why you do something, and what you do to counteract the opposing team's plays.

Another chapter of my education in thinking like a coach came in the winter of 1934, also when I was 14. The junior high school coach was A.N. "Tony" Lockyear, an excellent teacher of fundamentals, a disciplinarian, and a practitioner of strong defense. We had some marvelous defensive efforts that year. We held one team scoreless, and we defeated another team 40-1.

My error in judgment cost us a shutout in that 40-1 game. At halftime, it was 22-0, and Coach Lockyear said he wanted us to play well in the second half, but he added that he didn't necessarily want to shut out this team because the opposing coach was a good friend of his. With three seconds to go, the score was 40-0. At that point, I remembered his halftime talk, and committed an unnecessary foul that allowed the other team its single point in a

40-1 game. I thought I had done the coach a favor, but in the dressing room after the game, I realized that wasn't the case. From Coach Lockyear's diatribe, I learned two things: First, you never allow an opponent an easy score, and second, defense is paramount in a basketball game.

Even in that era, we played football games on Friday nights. Lights weren't used for major-league baseball until the late 1930s, but we started to use them earlier on high school football fields. Many projects were done for sports in those days by the Works Progress Administration, as a result of the Depression.

The College Recruiters

Going back to those days, 53 years ago, you might think that college recruiting was a phenomenon yet to be experienced. Not so. Certainly recruiting is a different game today, what with jet travel and a passel of different rules, but the essence of the practice was established even then.

I think I was contacted by about 70 schools in 1937 as an athletic prospect. Some contact was made by mail, but I'd say 75 percent or more was done through personal meetings in my home. The difference between then and now is recruiting took more time then. Coaches travelled by train, and to get to a player's home in the middle of the country was tough. Yet, I can tell you a recruiting story that might not sound so different from those of today.

From those 70, I cut the list to three schools—Kansas, Northwestern, and Stanford. In those days, schools offered what you might call a working scholarship. You might get tuition and books or something like that, but a scholarship was based strictly on academics at some schools, such as Northwestern and Stanford. In addition to tuition and books, you often would be lined up with a job to help put you through school.

My father and uncle were graduates of Kansas, so the school had always been a favorite with me. I went to Chicago by train to visit Northwestern, but Chicago was out of my class, the big, windy city. Too big for me.

I do remember getting an education on the way. After dinner—my first in a dining car—they brought me a silver bowl with white liquid. I didn't know what to do with it. Well, there were two older ladies across the way, the only other people in the dining car at that time. They were eating considerably later than I, but I decided I was going to learn what I should do with this bowl. So I waited until theirs arrived, and they dipped their fingers in and washed their hands. Who'd ever heard of anything like that?

I still had to decide between Kansas and Stanford, and that's where it started getting sticky. John Bunn was the coach at Stanford, a former player of my college coach, Dr. Forrest C. "Phog" Allen. Bunn hailed from Humboldt, Kansas, about nine miles from Chanute, and he had been a high school friend of my father as well as a teammate of my uncle Howard at Kansas under Dr. Allen. As coach at Stanford, Bunn happened to attend the Kansas high school tournament my sophomore year, when I set my record of 83 points in the tournament. I was 15 then, but he kept track through the years.

I wasn't going to visit Stanford. It was just too far away. But I was working in the summertime at a filling station following my senior year, and a Stanford alumnus came by and offered a trip out to Stanford. I didn't like my job very much so I said fine.

I took the train to Los Angeles and met a group of Stanford athletes, who entertained me for an afternoon and an evening, and then sent me on up to Palo Alto, where I met the famed Hank Luisetti. They did a good job, let's put it that way. I ended up in a hot box at 2:00 a.m., and finally I said, "OK, OK, I'll come to Stanford."

They wanted me to stay there, without returning to Chanute. Luisetti asked me to go deer hunting with him up in Washington, which would have been a new experience. The alumni presented several nice reasons why I shouldn't go home, but I told John Bunn, "I've got to go back and tell my folks I've decided to go to Stanford."

I felt it was only right that I should tell my parents face-to-face. John happened to be coming back to Kansas City for two weeks to do a promotional film about basketball so he decided he would drive me back to Chanute. Of course, this would be illegal today.

Ironically, the trip backfired on John because you have a great deal of time for conversation on a four-day trip. During the trip, he informed me it would be wise for me to come to Stanford and play football my first year, but then I should concentrate on basketball. Well, that comment turned me off, because I liked football just as much as basketball. That was the first inkling I had that maybe I'd made a hasty decision. In the meantime, John promised to take me back to Stanford in two weeks.

About a day after I got home, Gwinn Henry, the athletic director at Kansas, and Ad Lindsey, the football coach, showed up at my house. I'm sure my dad had informed them I had changed my mind. We had a nice visit and they concluded it by saying Dr. Allen wanted to talk to me, but he was in Indiana where his son, Bobby, was going to military school for the summer. So they suggested driving me back to Lawrence, then putting me on the train to Chicago, where I'd meet Dr. Allen and then attend a college football all-star game. My girlfriend from Chanute also happened to be there. Her father worked for the Santa Fe and she had a rail pass.

We drove all the way back to Lawrence from Chicago and Dr. Allen was very persuasive. I had just gotten back to Lawrence when the telephone rang. It was my father. "What are you going to do?" he wanted to know.

I said, "Well, dad, I've changed my mind again."

He said that was fine but John Bunn was going to be there at 3:00 that afternoon to pick me up. "I'm not going to tell him you've decided to stay here," my dad said. "You come tell him."

When Dr. Allen heard that, he took me back to Chanute. He fully intended to be there during the discussion with John Bunn. So we walked into the living room and there was John. Now Dr. Allen was quite influential in getting John the job at Stanford and they'd been friends a long time.

Dr. Allen started off, "You know, John, we're friends. I helped you get the job at Stanford. Now you have 47 states in which to recruit and you don't have to come into Kansas."

John started his rebuttal, and I decided it was time to get out of there. I came back about an hour later. It wasn't exactly a friendly confrontation. My dad said, "For the last time, tell these two gentlemen what you are going to do."

So I said, "I'm sorry, John, but I have decided to go to Kansas University."

And I did. As I've always said, not much has changed about the game of basketball—including recruiting—in the last 60 years.

3

Rock Chalk Jayhawk

I never regretted attending Kansas. Granted, my years in football were hard ones; we never had a winning season. Yet, in terms of preparation for my profession, I couldn't have done better.

So much of basketball originated in Kansas. The first coach at Kansas University (KU), was Dr. Naismith, who ironically, was the school's most unsuccessful coach—he had a nine-year record of 55-60. Of course, as we will see, he intended the game for more modest purposes than record keeping.

Then there was Dr. Allen, one of the game's true giants. He coached at Kansas for 39 years in two stints from 1907 to 1956 and recorded 771 victories, second on the all-time list to Adolph Rupp of Kentucky, who played for Dr. Allen. Today the man whose age and total victories combine to make him a logical candidate to surpass the legendary Rupp's 875 wins is North Carolina's Dean Smith — another protegé of Dr. Allen. More evidence of his legacy is a large number of former players and coaches now in the Naismith Hall of Fame.

Kansas Football

Football was another matter. Kansas had had a couple of winning seasons early in the 1930s before slipping to 1-6-1 in 1936. The year I went in, they were going to rebuild football. We had more than 90 recruits on the freshman team, which was legal in those days. And they weren't bad. In fact, after about three days of practice, we played the varsity and got whipped badly.

About three weeks later, Coach Lindsey brought the freshmen up for fodder and we kicked the varsity, and kicked them rather badly. That was the last time we were ever invited up to play the varsity.

In 1938, my sophomore year, we opened with a win over Texas, and then went back to play Notre Dame. We were feeling great. We felt we could beat Notre Dame. We really didn't have a bad football team. Well, we got beat 52-0. It was just a terrible, terrible shot to get beat like that. I was so embarrassed. Paul Masoner was a fraternity brother of mine and also a quarterback. He lived in Kansas City so we talked Coach Lindsey into letting us off there so we could go visit Paul's parents. We didn't want to have to go back on the same damn train and be met after getting whomped 52-0.

As it turned out, redemption came quickly. Our next game was against Washburn University of Topeka. I threw five touchdown passes, and we won 58-14. Somehow, five TD passes has stood up through the years, and it's still in the KU record books. Funny thing, I didn't think too much about it. In fact, one of the big shocks I got a few years ago was watching a UCLA-Nebraska game, and the announcer said Steve Taylor of Nebraska had tied the conference record for touchdown passes held jointly by Ralph Miller. I didn't even know it was a record.

Today the only difficulty I have is making people believe Washburn was a Division I school. They were members of the Missouri Valley Conference back in those days, and as time went on, they dropped down. But I could always throw the ball and throw it well. If a man got open, it was my job to get the ball to him. My passing percentage was highest in the nation in 1939.

Red Smith, writing in the *Philadelphia Record*, Sept. 27, 1941: "Temple opened Philadelphia's college football season last night with the tender care of a bride opening a can for the first home-cooked meal, and the contents proved a tasty dish for 23,000 spectators.

"Right under the lid was a 31-9 victory over the air-minded Jayhawkers of the University of Kansas, a nifty troupe of Fancy Dans led by one

of the handiest forward passers this town ever
saw.

"This character, a rangy, lantern-jawed
prairie kid named Ralph Miller, kept an outmanned and overpowered Kansas team in the
ball game with his alarmingly accurate side-
armed pitching . . ."

Football also gave me an injury that would have a profound
effect on my college career. At Ames, Iowa, in 1938, we were
playing Iowa State when I broke loose with a clear field for a
touchdown — clear, except that it was snowing, and I had one
defender to beat.

All I had to do was cut back and prance in for a touchdown,
but as I put my foot down, my knee gave way. It proved to be a
nagging problem for a long time although I played two more
games of the football season and all of the basketball season that
year. Still, loose cartilage would cause the knee to pop out on me
17 different times before two surgeries finally corrected it.

One of those occasions was the basketball season of 1938-
1939. We had a game at Manhattan against Kansas State, and that
cartilage was stuck. The knee was virtually locked. Dr. Allen was
kind enough to take me on the trip anyway. I didn't take a
uniform because I wasn't going to be able to play. Well, there was
an old hotel there, the Gillette Hotel, and we were going out for
our normal walk of a mile or so. The Gillette Hotel had four steps
that you had to go down to get to the street. I limped along and
as is common when one has such an injury, I swung my leg out.
I came to the first step, swung my leg on the ground, and pop, the
knee went back into place. We had to borrow a uniform, and
Kansas State furnished me a pair of shoes. I played 40 minutes
that night.

Finally, I underwent surgery in the summer of 1939 to remove
cartilage on the inside of the knee, thinking that would cure the
problem. However, it still popped out on me, so the spring of
1940 brought a second surgery to take out the outside cartilage.
That meant that I wouldn't graduate in 1941 with my class, but in
1942, because the doctor felt I had to be off the knee for a year to
let the damage heal. I suppose you could say that the 1940-1941

school year was a benchmark for me because that was my introduction to coaching, modest as the circumstances were.

Mt. Oread High School was right there on the Kansas campus, a school populated mostly by the sons and daughters of professors. As part of my practice teaching, I was appointed basketball coach. It was not grandiose. There were perhaps 40 or 45 students in the place, maybe 15 or 16 boys. As professors' sons, they tended to be highly intelligent, but not endowed with an abundance of physical talent. I don't recall that we fared very well.

Besides passing, one of the things in which I took great pride was my punting. As a senior in 1941, I led the nation in punting by several yards going into our last three games. Unfortunately, the last three games were played in mud, and that took me out of the national lead. The bounces were few and far between in the mud. Artificial turf was a quarter-century away.

My last college game, against Missouri, was somewhat typical. We went out and spray-painted the football field. The grass would always turn brown so we painted the field. It was the nicest-looking field in the Midwest when we finished it on Friday. Saturday about noon, the clouds came up. At 12:10 p.m. it started raining. Thirty minutes before the game, it started snowing and the snow and rain never stopped. The field was like a pig sty.

It was a long day —we got beat 45-6. I got tired of chasing Harry Ice and Robert Steuber, Missouri's All-Big Six backs, from one side of the field to the other. Finally, I intercepted a lateral in the backfield from my safety position and went about 40 yards for a touchdown, but I was so dirty, nobody knew who it was. The radio announcers gave the touchdown to my brother Dick.

We went in at halftime and got to put on new jerseys. They never felt so good, but the clean feeling didn't last. At the start of the second half, I ran the kickoff back, and two guys knocked me back into the biggest ice puddle you can imagine. I got up and my teeth were chattering. They didn't stop until 8:00 that night. We had steam heat in my fraternity house and I sat on a radiator until my shivering ceased. It was all representative of some long afternoons of football at KU.

Basketball From the Beginning

Our fortunes were much different in basketball. During my junior season of 1939-1940, we went 19-6, won a Big Six playoff game with Oklahoma, and won a district playoff with Henry Iba's Oklahoma A&M team. Then, in the NCAA's second national tournament, we took the Western Regional with victories over Rice and Southern California. Indiana, however, brought it all to a halt in the national championship game, beating us 60-42 at Kansas City.

I sat out the next year before coming back for my senior season. We finished at 17-5, playing in the Western Regional again and coming up two points short to Colorado in the first game. The knee was healed by now and I was able to make the All-Big Six first team.

> *Wichita Beacon*, Feb. 3, 1942: "A Kansas University basketball hero who less than a year ago was placed on the shelf and tagged 'through' because of a football knee injury, staged a one-man show at the Forum Monday night before a crowd of 3,000 persons to score 30 points and lead Kansas to a 56-37 triumph over the University of Wichita Shockers . . .
>
> "The young man is senior Ralph Miller, a shot-maker par excellence from Chanute who turned in the dizziest shooting performance imaginable as he hit baskets from all angles and distances. One basket was actually converted from the prone position . . . Miller's record not only shattered the mark for the Forum, but it broke the Kansas record as well."

The driving force behind KU basketball, of course, was Dr. Allen, truly one of basketball's legendary figures. Where does one begin to discuss him? Well, perhaps with his own college coach, Dr. James Naismith.

After inventing the game in 1891, Dr. Naismith joined the faculty at KU in 1898 as a member of the physical education department as well as university chaplain. When he invented the game, Dr. Naismith intended it only for recreational purposes. If he could see the sprinting, soaring, baseline-to-baseline game of today, I'm sure he would be shocked. Certainly, he never had in mind any sort of demanding sport, nor did he foresee any cerebral, chess-match sort of strategy to it. He was Kansas' first coach in the season of 1898-1899, winning seven and losing four. He coached through the 1907 season, but when Dr. Allen—who played for him from 1905-1907—told him he was thinking about a career in coaching, Naismith replied, "You don't coach basketball, Forrest, you play it."

Fortunately, Dr. Allen didn't heed his advice.

I would describe Dr. Naismith as a gentleman of the old school—celluloid collar, neat, trim, always well dressed. He was somebody you respected. He was an ordained minister with deep religious beliefs. I listened to some of his lectures, which were in kinesiology and related subjects.

Dr. Naismith left the development of basketball to other people, except to make a concerted effort to see that the game did not become too strenuous. For instance, he bitterly opposed the benchmark rule of 1936 that took the center jump out of basketball, creating a far more strenuous game.

He retired from active teaching in 1937, the year I arrived at Kansas, but he continued to conduct experiments with the basketball players there. He would take people out of quick scrimmages after the elimination of the center jump and check their heartbeat. He was actually concerned about whether basketball players would die from the activity. He was known to have played the game he invented only three times. The first was in an exhibition game back at Springfield in 1891, the second was when he went to Denver and brought the game to a YMCA there, and the third was at Kansas in the late 1890s.

His belief about coaching really didn't change, from the time he handed the reins of the Kansas program to Dr. Allen in 1907 until his death in 1939 at 78 years. My association with him was very casual, just like any student with any professor who happened to be famous.

The Father of Basketball Coaching

Many people refer to Phog Allen as the father of basketball coaching, and I wouldn't have any reason to dispute it. He succeeded Dr. Naismith in 1907 for a period of two years and then returned in 1919 for a tenure that stretched all the way to 1956. Among his coaching assignments was that of directing a professional team, the Kansas City Germans. He was a player/coach and the other starters on the team were his brothers.

He was a doctor of osteology, an innovator, a motivator. He developed the greatest trainers during the 1920s, 1930s, and 1940s, and he was something of a pioneer in athletic medicine, combining two fields.

Dr. Allen designed his own basketball shoes. He advocated use of the 12-foot basket, something I think should have entered the game long ago. He invented a game called "goal high," introduced late in the 1930s and rather popular during World War II. You had a standard with a little iron hoop, no backboard. They sold a lot of them to the military because they were easy to handle.

Dr. Allen was also one of the founders of the National Association of Basketball Coaches, as well as a driving force behind inclusion of basketball in the Olympic Games. The Games were in Los Angeles in 1932. With the host country allowed to add a new sport, there was much consideration given to adding basketball at that time, but it didn't make it. Basketball did become part of the Games at the 1936 Olympics in Berlin.

One of the sidelights of the 1936 Games was that Dr. Naismith saw the introduction of the game he invented into the Olympics. He had received much fame, but surely no money for creating the game, so at every high school, college, and AAU game of the 1935-1936 season, a penny of all charged admissions went toward a fund to send him and his wife to Berlin. Enough money was raised for the trip and for plenty of spending money for the Naismiths.

Dr. Allen could remember your name if he met you once. Until an unfortunate accident in the season of 1945-1946, he was uncanny in his ability to remember details. He was having a practice one day that year and happened to be wearing street clothes because of a speech he was giving that evening in Topeka. His Kansas team was scrimmaging and one of his biggest players was running downcourt, full-speed. He collided with Dr. Allen, who hit the back of his head on the floor.

Dr. Allen was stunned, but got up and thought nothing more of it at the time. However, a few weeks later some problems arose. Dr. Allen called his son Bob—who was then interning at the university hospital—and told him he was having severe headaches. After a thorough examination, doctors discovered he had suffered a severe concussion, and he didn't coach the rest of that season. He did return the following season, but his memory was blurred for some time.

Dr. Allen loved big words. He called our defense the "stratified transitional man-to-man defense with a zone principle." He did have his quirks, many of them related to motivation. One time we were playing at Stillwater against one of Henry Iba's Oklahoma A&M teams. We played what we called a three-out, two-in type of offense, the two-in being essentially post players—not as we know postmen today.

We got into a situation where we thought it would be of benefit to have a postman. So after returning from the trip, the team selected me to go talk to Doc, which I did. I made my little speech and Doc said, "Well, Ralph, we're already using the best offense there is."

He had a professorial manner that said you'd better be prepared when you made a plea like this. I said, "I don't argue that, Doctor."

I left and went to practice. That night, Dr. Allen said, "I understand some of the team thinks we should have a postman."

Then he put four good athletes with me and said, "You fellows know how to run a single-post offense. We're going to scrimmage, and you men use the single-post, and the other team is going to use my offense, the one we use. And we'll see who wins."

We scrimmaged for two hours. The single-post team was never behind. He had a whole squad and was substituting freely. The five of us were it. Finally after two hours, they tied us. Whistle blew, and Dr. Allen said sternly, "All right, gentlemen, the next team that scores a basket wins."

I said, "Doc, can we have one timeout?"

He consented. I got our group together and said, "We have the ball. Whoever gets an open shot, take it — if we make it, we win. If we miss it, I don't want to see anybody cover his man. Personally, I'm a little tired."

Well, fortunately, we made the bucket and Doc said, "All right, that's all, gentlemen."

The subject was never brought up again until after the final regular-season game. We played Oklahoma at Norman the last game of the regular season and lost. On the train coming back, Dr. Allen said, "I want to see my starting five in my stateroom."

We joined him and he said, "Gentlemen, I think we are going to have to make a slight change in the offense. We're going to have to have a postman. What do you think?"

"Doc, you know what I think," I said.

"Fine, Ralph, you're the postman."

Well, we had only one light practice before the final game of the NCAA tournament, so we never worked on the single-post offense. We'd had a very long, tough finish to the season. The loss at Oklahoma created a three-way tie in the Big Six between Oklahoma, Kansas, and Missouri, forcing a playoff at Wichita. Kansas won that and went on to beat Oklahoma State in the regional at Oklahoma City.

But we used the single-post throughout the tournament, and from that time on, Kansas used a single-post offense. That was the way Dr. Allen worked — unorthodox, unpredictable, but usually very effective.

On another occasion, we were going to play at Kansas State, and Doc sensed that perhaps we were a little overconfident. So he had us line up, facing each other. The first two in line were Bob Allen, his son, and me. Doc says, "Now Ralph, I want you to slap Bob. You heard me, slap him."

So I did. He wanted me to do it harder. And we went down the line, slapping each other. Another means of motivation, Dr. Allen-style.

His reading must have been correct, because we were trailing late in the game. He called timeout, called us over and said, "All right, gentlemen, we are going to have to fast-break."

"What?" we said. We never fast-broke.

"We're going to fast-break, we're going to have to to win this game. You know how to do it, now do it!"

We did. And we won. That was Doc.

He also had some rituals, and there would be no deviation.

Throughout my career, I would take an afternoon nap before games, and I suppose it stemmed from playing under Dr. Allen. We always took a nap, got up and took a two-mile walk.

There was the other tradition that I didn't particularly enjoy—tea and toast. Dr. Allen held firmly to the notion that there were certain things suitable for pre-game and post-game consumption. Before games, it was always hot tea, toast, and fruit. After games, it was cereal and ice cream, no red meat. Well, the team got tired of this after awhile, and as usual, I found myself in the role of spokesman.

"Doc," I said, "We're getting tired of cereal and milk and ice cream after a game. Can't we have a hamburger once in a while?"

All of a sudden, we could have a hamburger. He was a disciplinarian, but he could adjust.

The Tradition

When I first began college coaching at Wichita in 1951, I was a devotee of the Allen approach on tea and toast. But the final 35 years or so of my career, my players were spared that rite, and for that, they can thank Bill Russell, K.C. Jones, and the devastating team Phil Woolpert put together at the University of San Francisco in the mid-1950s.

We played in the first round of the All-College Tournament at Oklahoma City in December of 1954. Our Wichita State team and San Francisco were staying out at the OCU campus in dormitories built out of World War II barracks. This particular year we were the No. 1-seeded team in the tournament, and San Francisco was No. 8, so we drew them as our first opponent.

We went in and we were having our little tea and toast. Of course, as per Dr. Allen's philosophy, there was no milk before a game. We're dilly-dallying with our tea and toast and honey, and here comes USF. They've loaded their trays with fried chicken and steaks, four or five glasses of milk, pie a la mode. My kids were sitting there wondering whether their coach was very smart.

Well, I learned two things from that: One, it doesn't much matter what you eat before a game. And second, I discovered how valuable somebody like Bill Russell is.

My brother Dick, who was my assistant coach, had gone to

Los Angeles to scout USF against UCLA. He came back thoroughly impressed with Bill Russell, but he also said it looked like USF's weakness was outside shooting. So we dropped back into a zone.

USF proceeded to hit nine shots in a row from outside.

I looked down at my brother and said, "Where did you see this outfit play?"

About that time, they missed. The ball hit the back of the rim, went clear above the backboard, so Russell puts his hand on top of the ball and slams it down through the hoop. I'd never seen this before — and neither had Cleo Littleton, our best player. He was crouching down under the basket and Bill's shot hit him square in the nose and bounced into the bleachers.

I called timeout and I said, "Well, gang, this can't go on." I was correct. It only lasted 40 minutes.

We got beat 94-75. So one of Dr. Allen's pet habits was jettisoned. After all, Cleo Littleton, the first player west of the Mississippi to score 2,000 points, always liked to have two chili dogs and two colas before a game. Who was I to argue?

Courtship and Marriage

It was at Kansas where fate smiled on me and I met a certain girl named Emily Jean Milam. She was from Topeka and entered school in 1938, a year after I did. In those days, most classes seated you alphabetically, so in physiology class, we ended up sitting next to each other and we became acquainted.

Jean came to our fraternity dance with someone else that Christmas. I decided I was going to get serious about her, and I did. I began courting her and gave her my pin by the spring session.

She lived in a house that was right on the back of a wheatfield south of the campus. Well, one day, she got mad at me, took off the pin and threw it over the fence. Talk about a needle in a haystack. I knew hunting for it was a lost cause. So I had to buy her more than one pin.

But it all worked out well. On September 5, 1942, a few months after each of us had graduated, we were married. No question, it was the nicest thing that ever happened to me.

4

Finding My Game Plan

I came out of college with no intention of coaching. Certainly my little stint at Mt. Oread hadn't produced much. We might have won one or two games, if that. The experience had stimulated no desire in me to be a coach. Both Jean and I went to work for Aero Parts in Wichita. Jean was an assistant secretary to the president of the company. I signed on with the company's semi-pro football team. We played teams like the old Cleveland Browns and Chicago Cardinals.

My Career Search

World War II was heating up. The draft lottery was in effect. My number was 40, so I was called up immediately, but because I'd had problems with my back as well as my knee, the Navy wouldn't let me in. I went through a couple of reclassifications during the time I was personnel manager at Aero Parts, and finally I thought, "Why don't I go take the physical?"

A funny thing happened when I took it. One doctor said, "You didn't have this knee operated on."

"Let me ask you a question," I said. "Is this your field?"

"Yes," he said.

"Well, then you should know the name C.B. Francisco." He was one of the specialists at that time.

"Those are the smallest scars I've ever seen," the doctor said.

Indeed, they were small scars, but I was able to convince them that I had had two knee surgeries. So I entered the Air Force. I was inducted at Fort Leavenworth, Kansas, and headed for basic training at Wichita Falls, Texas. There I ran into kind of a smart-aleck corporal who taught me that college sports were of great value.

"What do you want to do?" he asked.

"Well, I'm a graduate in physical education," I said, "so I'd like to get into physical training."

"That's all filled up," he said. "All we've got left is radio and gunners."

"I don't know anything about either one of them," I said.

In the meantime, he's scanning through my papers and sees that I had played football and basketball at Kansas. So he goes over to the lieutenant, comes back and says, "You're in physical training. Shut your mouth and take it."

And I did.

I was lucky. I didn't have to go overseas, and Jean was able to be with me all of my 37 months in the service, except for a few months when I was in Officer Candidate School (OCS) in San Antonio. I coached the basketball team every place I went. It was really kind of an enjoyable life. We didn't have to face the peril that others did during the war.

After graduation from OCS, I was assigned to Drew Field in Tampa. By now, Jean's family had all moved to Redlands, California, and I was transferred to the Fourth Air Force in California, because of a man named Major E.B. DeGroot, who had been one of my professors at Kansas. He headed the Fourth Air Force Division there. I dropped him a letter and said that if he had any openings in the Fourth Air Force, I'd appreciate getting picked up. He wrote back to tell me about an opening. After I got to his office in San Francisco, I found out quickly where the need was.

"You know," he said, "I just lost my quarterback." That was Jake Leicht, formerly of the University of Oregon and later a Pac-10 football official.

"That's fine," I said. "I haven't been on the football field for four years and I'm not interested in going back."

That didn't make a difference. He needed a quarterback.

"What if I don't want to be a quarterback?" I asked.

Well, he said, I had two choices. I could join the Fourth Air Force football team in Ontario and be a quarterback. Or if I didn't want to be a quarterback, the only other option was a base in Washington with which I was unfamiliar.

He had made his point. I went to the Fourth, joined the football team, and played on it for about two weeks. During that span, our first child, Susan, was born to us, and at the same time, the team lost an important game that would prevent it from winning the service championship. I called Mr. DeGroot, and said, "Look, you've got some fine young players and you can't win the championship. I really am too far out of shape to do your team any good."

He relieved me of my duties and assigned me to March Air Force Base in Riverside. There I became the basketball coach for the Fourth Air Force team.

I was discharged in April of 1946. By that time, we had two children, Susan and Cappy.

A word about that name Cappy. My father had been a thespian. Back in the earlier years at Chanute, the faculty always used to put on a series of plays associated with a character named Cappy Ricks. My father played Cappy Ricks, so the students named him that. When I came into the picture, I became Little Cappy. People at Kansas, even the newspapers, referred to me as Cappy. Our oldest son's name was Ralph, and we gave him the nickname Cappy, too, but he preferred Ralph.

The Big Fortune

I was 27 years old and still unsure about a career. I surely didn't envision coaching as a profession. My first job out of the service was as assistant director of the Redlands Recreation Department. It was about that time that I thought I had a great opportunity to become a millionaire by being a wholesale fruit distributor. Well, I didn't become a millionaire; in fact, I became a pauper in a hurry.

This was the winter of 1947-1948. The previous year, I had been contacted by the Wichita Public School System in a round-about way. Someone wanted to know if I would consider coaching basketball at Wichita North High School. I said, "No, I'm on my way to making a fortune."

That lasted almost to Christmas time. We had to buy a truck for the business and the payments were strapping us severely.

The Alpha Beta grocery chain pulled out of the group to which we were supplying fruit. Suddenly, I found myself with a wife, two children, and no job.

There wasn't any work to be found in California. I did seek an assistant basketball coaching position at Pepperdine, but was unsuccessful. I simply couldn't find a job.

About this time, my father was contacted by an old friend, George Trombold, wanting to know if I would consider going back to Wichita East High School shortly before the end of the 1947-1948 season. Emmett Breen had quit the job there to become a backfield coach at his alma mater, Kansas State.

There could be no other answer but yes. In mid-February, 1948, my coaching days effectively began at East High School. I was happy to be working.

High School Coaching and the 2-2-1

Off I was, then, to a career that would carry through 41 years— five decades, and very close to a sixth. I can't say I was well-equipped to coach at that time, but then again, I probably knew as much about the game as many of the people who were coaching.

My entry into the game was unusual in that I was heading into a situation where there were only about five weeks left on the schedule. So there wasn't much time to assess talent or to concoct new offenses or defenses. Fortunately, my assistant, Frank Henkel, had been there since 1943 and had a good handle on our personnel.

> **Frank Henkel: "We had used a single-post offense before the coaching change. Old Phog Allen had used a double-post offense some at Kansas, so on our first night of practice after Ralph got the job, Ralph sets up the double post. God, the players were so confused, they didn't know what was going on.**
>
> **"So Ralph says, OK, OK, and tells them to go shoot free throws. We went off to a hallway**

and Ralph had a smoke. We went back in and
Ralph told them to get in the single-post offense.
All of a sudden, they just started hitting. You
know what, he never played a double post the
rest of his coaching days there. I can't remember
him using it in college, either."

Soon after my arrival back in Kansas, I discovered a major
change had taken place since I had left. The 2-2-1, full-court
pressure defense had sprung up at many high schools. It was
totally foreign to me.

During the five weeks before the end of that season, we only
had to play one team that utilized the 2-2-1, and we were beaten
pretty soundly. That team was Lawrence, and its personnel
certainly wasn't superior to ours. In preparing for that one game,
we gave our junior varsity the 2-2-1 for practice purposes and we
could see that it was bothering our varsity more than it should.
That group certainly wasn't as talented as the varsity.

I was intrigued, but we didn't use the 2-2-1 in 1948. We played
out the string that season using the system that Breen had
employed. I spent part of the summer of 1948 gathering information on the 2-2-1. I liked it.

I sought out Cade Sur‑ ‑, who had won two state championships at Wellington, Kansas, and was then coach at Fort Hays
Teachers College. He was a very, very fine teacher. He told me all
I needed to know, and the more I heard, the more interested I
became. Understand that the 2-2-1 was still considered a gimmick in those days. The teams that ran it only did so in specific
situations, not for an entire game.

After listening to Cade, I said, "Look, I was always taught that
if a defense is good enough to use at all, it should be sound
enough to use all the time. Why doesn't that happen with the 2-
2-1?"

"First of all," Cade said, "you understand that to have the
zone position, you have to have time to establish your floor
position, so if you don't score, there's no time to set up your
formation."

"That's understandable," I said, "but still, if you like pressure and use pressure, why do you use it only half the time?"

"Well," he said, "I don't have an answer for that one. I guess maybe it's because nobody's ever thought about it before."

Some background on the 2-2-1 is in order. To my knowledge, Gene Johnson introduced the 2-2-1, at least in the United States—Gene got the idea from Mexico. Gene Johnson was the coach at Wichita University from 1928 to 1933. In the summer of 1931 the team took a tour of Mexico and discovered that clubs there played a radically new style of ball that differed greatly from the control style used in the U.S.

The Americans had an advantage in height and size, but the Mexicans harassed the ball-handler at all times. This was something new for Wichita. The team didn't lose too many games, but found its offense totally disrupted by this newfangled defense.

Gene Johnson: "I came to the conclusion that if a bunch of smaller men like those on the Mexican teams could upset a team of taller men like mine, why couldn't I take that type of game, harass the team that had the ball, but still keep some safety people back? If I could take that wild type of game and upset my opponents, yet keep it so they couldn't get (layups) on us, we'd be successful.

"All the other teams in the United States played slow-break basketball, passing the ball back and forth and back and forth, until you got your men situated. My theory was, when they brought the ball down and stopped, we went right out and attacked them. We always had the other team's balance upset, because we were the only team in the United States that played that kind of basketball. Even though they knew what we were going to do, they couldn't do anything against us because they weren't used to that kind of basketball.

"Hank Iba decided he wouldn't play my team anymore. He told me that if he tried to get

his team ready to play me, it would upset his team the rest of the season.

"I left Wichita and coached the MacPherson Oilers to the national title in 1936. When I left, some of the sportswriters said, 'Well, your system's good against the college boys, but these old pros and the AAU, they won't do the dumb tricks the college boys have been doing.' I said we'll wait and see.

"In the past 20 years teams have gradually been playing more fast-break basketball. Now the professional teams and most of the good college teams play wild and woolly. They don't put the press on like we did, but they still force the game into a fast and furious pace."

I used to have sportswriters rolling their eyes when I told them that essentially nothing about the game had changed in the past 60 years. But it's true. Wichita was bothering offenses with the 2-2-1 back in the early 1930s, some 30 years before John Wooden's slick UCLA teams began terrorizing people in the early 1960s.

How did the 2-2-1 stay secret for so long? Well, it wasn't exactly unknown, but it was totally foreign outside Kansas. Understand, Wichita was a small school, certainly dwarfed in size and reputation by Kansas and Kansas State. And the 2-2-1— among those even aware of it—was viewed as a gimmick.

Gene Johnson became an assistant coach of the first U.S. Olympic basketball team in 1936. Shortly after that he was named head coach at Kansas Wesleyan University in Salina. Out of that came a group of disciples of the 2-2-1. Many of them were Kansas high school coaches. Some of them, like Cade Suran, went on to win state championships, yet the defense really didn't gain widespread acceptance. The 2-2-1 was buried in the state of Kansas for a long time. It's always been amazing to me that something as effective as the 2-2-1 stayed a secret for 20 years.

I think it's too bad that nobody has ever given Gene Johnson credit for what he did for college basketball. He brought in something in 1932 that is still being used 58 years later, yet few people today know his name. John Wooden is sometimes given credit for the 2-2-1, but the origination of the defense in the U.S. can be traced to Gene Johnson.

Now let's put the 2-2-1 in perspective with the ebb and flow of offense and defense of that era. The concepts set down by Gene Johnson conquered, or at least suppressed, the advantages of the jump shot in basketball, popularized by Stanford University under Everett Dean. In the late 1930s, Hank Luisetti's one-handed shot became the forerunner of the jump shot. By the early 1940s, Luisetti was gone from Stanford, but the shot revolutionized the game, and Stanford won a national championship with it under Everett Dean in 1942.

It was earth-shaking. Young kids suddenly were shooting the jump shot. Defenses had no answer. The scores in high school and college became astronomical. Numbers up in the 100s were not uncommon. Particularly in the late 1940s, offense ruled the roost. People like Henry Iba, a great defensive tactician, were concerned that basketball might just become an exhibition type of activity rather than competitive.

However, by the mid-1950s, principles of pressure established within the framework of the 2-2-1 proved to be an antidote for all the scoring. All known pressure coverage stems from the fundamentals of the 2-2-1.

This is how slowly the 2-2-1 came to favor: Dr. Allen at Kansas approached me after the 1950-1951 season when we had won the state high school championship with it. Here was a renowned, veteran coach quizzing me — just starting my tenure at Wichita — about the nuances of the 2-2-1. He was curious about the principles and we brainstormed for three or four hours on the subject. Until then he had never used organized, pressure defenses.

As a result, the first team to use pressure defense on the national scene was Kansas in 1951-1952. That season Dr. Allen introduced his half-court man-to-man defense, a direct descendant of the 2-2-1. Kansas won the national championship with it, although the effect of the new defense was obscured by KU's Clyde Lovellette, a dominating center. It wasn't until 1953, when Kansas reached the national finals with just one starter returning from the 1952 team, that the world of basketball coaches began to think there was something special about this defense.

After meeting with Cade Suran, I got together with Frank Henkel and began plotting how the 2-2-1 could work for us. Our goal was to find a way to utilize the 2-2-1, and also use full-court pressure throughout the game.

We knew we couldn't use full-court zone defenses for every possession by the opponent because as Cade Suran pointed out, there isn't time to establish floor position after a missed attempt. But we recognized that defense, whether it was called man or zone, was really a combination of man and zone principles. We decided that all the basic concepts of the 2-2-1 could work very nicely with full-court man defenses. Out of this evolved our change-up theory of defense, a concept about as simple as it gets. If we made a basket on offense, we had time to establish zone floor position. If we missed or turned the ball over, however, we would always use man coverage.

We further manipulated our defenses so that we used both man and zone on half-court defense. We could start, for instance, with the full-court zone press, and drop back into man on the half-court, or vice versa. All these keys were established in pre-game talks or at halftime. Another principle we used immediately was matching defensive floor position with offensive floor position, so that it would add confusion and make it necessary for teams to think.

All of this fit hand-in-glove with a belief that I have long held about the essence of basketball. There is never time for thought out there—it has to be reflex. The game flows. One action creates a reaction. If players find themselves thinking too much, they'll be lost in a hurry. The game, especially played at the speed it is today, is simply too fast, too spontaneous.

I don't know how many times I've read these words from our opponents: "There were times when we didn't know what defense they were in." We have had opponents so confused that on occasion, they called four timeouts in a half. If the opposition had to spend that much time recognizing what we were doing, and then going about attacking it, we were already closer to victory. There were times when the force of indecision combined with a demon on perimeter defense, like Dwayne Allen at Oregon State, were devastating.

The key to the change-up was simply a make or a miss, which baffled not only our opponents on occasion, but many other people. I was attending a clinic one time, and a young man came up and said, "You know, Coach, I've been scouting your team for five years, I've watched you, and I can't figure out how you signal a defensive change. You don't hold up fingers, you're not holding up signs or anything."

In the broad perspective, what the 2-2-1 did was bring a dramatic reversal in philosophy to basketball. For a long time offense had always been accorded the privilege of attacking. It was an unwritten rule that the offense would initiate its action, and then the defense would react to that — much like allowing your opponent in chess to make his move before you retaliate. Therefore, offense always had a slight advantage.

That edge, combined with the burgeoning effect of the jump shot, swung the game to an offensive show. Defense lagged. But then came the 2-2-1, introducing not only a whole new set, but a philosophy of combating offense.

In concert with this we forwarded the idea that the 2-2-1 could cause opponents problems not only in scheme and in recognition, but in fatigue as well. What pressure did for basketball was create a game with two attacking forces, and what came of it was a more exciting brand of basketball.

Look at it this way: In a game, if each team has 60 possessions and neither one uses the fast-break or pressure defense, then usually five seconds will elapse from the time one team gets the ball until it begins its half-court possession. Multiply 120 possessions by five seconds, and you have 600 seconds, or ten minutes of a 40-minute game, which become resting time. With pressure, we're going to eliminate your rest periods.

Our full-court pressure was designed to create a span of fatigue, in which the offense would malfunction, often resulting in turnovers and easy baskets. Maybe it would last only two or three minutes, maybe it would occur only once in a game, but it frequently would lead to a telling stretch in which we would put together the run that won the game. Our victory over Purdue in 1970, clinching the Big Ten title in my last year at Iowa, was a perfect example of how it's supposed to work. We were eight or nine points down late in the first half and closed it down at halftime. Then in the last few minutes of the game, we came from eight or nine down and won.

I suppose what Loyola Marymount is doing nowadays—enticing opponents into a frantic, 94-foot game and taking advantage of superior conditioning—is a latter-day outgrowth of the concept.

Today, there is one great hindrance to the idea of creating fatigue in an opponent with full-court pressure: television. With 60- and 90-second television timeouts all the time, you simply don't have as much opportunity to make an opponent tired.

Like some other coaches—notably John Wooden and Dean Smith—I always hated to call a timeout, in part because of the aforementioned idea about not thinking on the floor. Again, a coach doesn't want players thinking too much. If the coach calls early timeouts, and you can get him thinking, what's going to happen to his players? One of the rare occasions when I violated that tenet was against Georgetown in our regional final game of 1982 when I called a timeout in the first three minutes. Unfortunately, it didn't help us.

Television has curtailed the need to call timeouts, especially early in the game. It has wrought havoc with the potential to tire an opponent. The primary purpose of our game execution was to eliminate rest periods. If there are four TV timeouts each half, and each coach happens to use up all four of his allotted timeouts—I see the rules committee has cut it back to three for the 1990-1991 season—that's 16 timeouts in a game. Who could get tired playing a 40-minute game with 16 timeouts?

State Champions

All of this makes sense, but I cannot say I was totally committed to the 2-2-1 by the time I began my first full season at Wichita East in 1948-1949. As a matter of fact, anybody reading the score of our first game that year might have thought we were trying to set the game back 40 years, not improve on it. Today, it's laughable, but at the time it wasn't so funny.

We were playing Arkansas City, a team in our conference, in our gym. At the end of the first quarter the score was Arkansas

City 2, East 0. No slowdown, no stall. That wasn't bad enough. At the half it was Arkansas City 4, East 0. I'd like to know how many coaches have ever walked into a halftime talk when they haven't scored a point. I can remember Frank Henkel looking at me as we were walking in and saying, "Don't get on 'em too bad, Ralph."

We were greatly encouraged at the opening tip of the third quarter. We scored, but at the end of the third quarter, the score was 7-2. Finally we won the ball game, 13-11. We took 48 shots, all of them decent, but they wouldn't go in the hole. The next day, Doc Allen sent me a telegram that said, "Congratulations on your newfangled control game."

At any rate, we didn't totally give way to the 2-2-1 at that time. We used it when we wanted. Our 1949 junior varsity became familiar with it because we were occasionally playing teams that used the 2-2-1. We wound up in the state tournament, facing a team that was supposed to beat us. We unveiled our 2-2-1, and it was like taking candy from a baby. Our East team went on to take second in the state.

More evidence. In 1950 we lost a game to Salina High School. They used the press and we didn't. I had to admit that my personnel was much better than theirs, yet we lost. The next year we won the state championship, the first at East since 1925.

> *Wichita Eagle,* **March 18, 1951: "In one year, Miller turned East into a ball of fire, a team proclaimed on all sides at Emporia by coaches, referees, and plain fans to be the fastest in state history.**
>
> **"There were some plays made in the semi-finals and finals which had the crowd gasping. We can recall a play late in the Parsons game in which players of each side fumbled the ball at mid-court, then little Lafayette Norwood, one of East's five colored boys, picked it up and before the crowd could follow the action, had flashed in for one of the slickest plays anyone ever saw.**
>
> **"Actually and literally, East's play was so fast that some fans just missed some of the scoring. That kind of basketball was too much for Newton, even an infallible passing team**

**drilled in many, many years of basketball tra-
dition. Whether or not it tends to an ending of
Newton's state mastery isn't sure, but sure as
shooting, it means an end to old-fashioned ball
possession. The fire-department stuff is clang-
ing, and man, how it does entertain 'em."**

That 1950-1951 team was one of the quickest, fastest teams
that had ever been seen in Kansas. In addition to a great scorer in
Cleo Littleton, I had an extremely quick guard, Charlie Gill.
Charlie was about 5' 5" and one of the greatest athletes I ever
knew.

He was a dude. Charlie was the best-dressed fellow in the
school. He came to school when he felt like it and rode in a taxi
cab. His senior year, he came out for football and he was the
greatest defensive safety I ever saw at East. They didn't use him
much on offense, but we were beating somebody pretty badly so
they let him play offense, and the first three times he got the ball,
he went 35, 55, and 75 yards for touchdowns.

Well, he came in after football season and said, "Coach, I'd
like to come out for basketball."

"You'd better be ready," I told him.

So we started practicing. Charlie didn't show up for about
four days. Finally he came in and said, "I'm ready now, Coach."

"Too bad, get out," I said.

"Aw, come on now, Coach," he said. "After football season,
I was tired. I had to take a little rest. I still want to come out for
basketball. I think I can make your team."

I finally consented. I had a tough time keeping him on the
bench, but I did for a month. Then, I put him in the starting lineup
and he didn't disappoint us. He had 17 points on seven of 11 field-
goal attempts in the championship game that year, and Cleo had
16.

We also had Lafayette Norwood, who would later become an
assistant coach at Kansas. Gill and Norwood were like lightning.
Later, Boeing Aircraft had a team and Charlie and Lafayette
became the two guards. I always liked to have my freshmen at
Wichita play them — what an education! These freshmen thought
they knew something about basketball. We'd just turn Charlie

and Lafayette loose. They were terrible to play against.

Linwood Burns, who was 6'3", Bobby Conn, and Rod Grubb rounded out that East team. It was a good one.

By then, I was an exponent of the 2-2-1, but I've always said you're constantly learning in this business, and there was one final straw that pushed me to total belief in the scheme. After I left East and went to Wichita University, we had a 27-4 season in 1954. I thought I was a pretty good coach. Maybe I had caught up with the big boys. I didn't have to use my 2-2-1. Many people still thought of it as a gimmick. Perhaps I even started to believe that.

Well, a few years later, in 1959, we hosted a good team from Los Angeles State and lost by the score of 106-101. Sax Elliott was the coach at LA State, and afterward, he said, "Ralph, you amaze me. You've been trying to sell me on this pressure game and I use it. I beat you and you don't even press. I don't understand it."

That was one of the nicest things anybody ever said to me. I thought to myself, "Well, you jerk, you've got a good thing here, and you didn't use it. And you lost another ball game."

From that day on, I used pressure defense.

I've always believed a coach will seldom make a decision on the bench that will turn the outcome of the game. The real secret of winning can be boiled down to preparation. Once in a blue moon you can make a suggestion during a game that might heavily influence it, but not very often. So what you try to do is prepare your team to play on its own.

We used this system 41 years. Counting service games, we won more than 700 games. Many personal honors came my way. I think that system was a lot of help. I think it's going to be effective for a long, long time.

Part II
Coaching at Wichita

5

Valley of Death

I was at home one evening in the spring of 1951 when the telephone rang. It was Dr. Harry Corbin, the president of Wichita University, inviting me for a personal chat that evening at his home. In about three hours, my life was changed. Dr. Corbin asked me if I would consider becoming the head basketball coach at the university. He said he had decided not to retain Ken Gunning, coach for the previous three seasons.

My answer to Dr. Corbin was yes, if he could meet one important condition: Add a full-time assistant coach. Until after World War II, few universities had full-time help for their head basketball coaches, and Wichita had never had a full-time assistant. I thought that if the school was going to compete successfully in the Missouri Valley Conference, it would need one.

Major Changes

For perspective, this era marked the beginning of hiring full-time assistants. In an earlier day, a basketball coach ran a program all by himself. The only help he might have would be a graduate assistant who might be working on an advanced degree. By about 1955, however, programs could have not only one, but two full-time assistants.

"How about Bob Kirkpatrick?" Dr. Corbin asked. Kirkpatrick had been a high school coach and was now in the physical education department at the university. He was a personal friend of mine.

"That's fine," I said, "if you'll relieve him from his full-time duties. I don't want an assistant obligated to a full course load."

As it turned out, Bob couldn't be relieved of his physical education position, because he was one of only two men in the physical education department at that time. However, I did get permission to add an assistant's position to the basketball staff. My first college assistant was my brother, Richard F. "Dick" Miller.

Dr. Corbin said he wanted to have some conversations with other people, but that he would get back to me the following day. He did call the next day to offer me the job. He proposed a salary of $5,000 and I snapped at it. It had always been my goal when I came out of college to make $5,000 a year. I figured if I made $5,000, I'd have it made for the rest of my life. Pales a little by today's standards, doesn't it? In fact, by the late 1950s, the salary had doubled and the university adopted a new retirement plan, one that had been advocated by our comptroller. It was designed to improve with each raise in pay.

"Who knows, Ralph," our comptroller said, "you may make $50,000 someday." I chuckled and told him he was a real dreamer.

There was one small hitch. Dr. Corbin wanted to keep the deal quiet for a couple of weeks so Ken Gunning could find another job. Well, it moved along nicely for about the first week. All was quiet. But one day right after that, Stub Mayo, the football coach at East, asked me, "Don't you ever tell your friends anything? What's this stuff that you've got the job at Wichita University?"

"Gosh," I said, "you must know more than I know."

Half an hour later, I get a call from the principal, Dr. Walter Cooper, asking me if it's true.

"Possibly," I said. I explained the situation and asked if he would keep it quiet.

"I think you ought to reconsider," he said.

"Mr. Cooper," I said, "a year ago I came to you and wanted a raise, because I'm at minimum. The coach across town makes over a thousand dollars a year more than I do. Yet I'm having success."

"Well, you know the tenure system." The city's tenure system provided for an annual raise of $100.

"I understand the system," I said. "but I also told you that I turned down a college job last spring."

I had been offered a chance to be football coach, basketball coach, and athletic director at Southwestern College in Winfield, Kansas. You were required to do many things in those days, especially at a smaller school.

"I also told you," I continued, "that it wouldn't be long until the next good offer came along, and I would take it. So really, we don't have anything more to discuss. This is an opportunity I'd really like to take and if it comes to pass, nothing you can say to me will make me stay at East."

Obviously, by then, the leak was out. It was all over town. Not only did Gunning leave, but the athletic director, Jim Trimble, quit because they went over his head. He didn't like the way the situation was handled—rightfully so—and he resigned.

Three years and a couple of months before the offer, I was a fruit distributor. Now at 32, I was going to be head coach of a college basketball team.

A Good Start

Wichita State, then known as Wichita University, was a small college school in athletics through the war. It had been known primarily for its football teams, which were quite good in the 1930s and 1940s. Basketball had been something that was just tolerated.

In 1947-1948, the school entered the Missouri Valley Conference and the world changed. You couldn't say there was much in the way of interest when I got there. The previous season Wichita had sold nine season tickets for basketball. Nine. Well, I said all the right things. There was a fair amount of anticipation among people thinking we could effect a quick turnaround, but I cautioned everyone that it was going to take time.

We got a good start without ever playing a game by recruiting Cleo Littleton, who would be able to stay in Wichita and play the same system he had grown up with in high school. Primarily a post player at 6' 3", he averaged 18.5 points a game that first year and we went 11-19. The first time I saw Cleo back at East, it was like looking at Gary Payton. I knew I had a player.

Paul Scheer was a sophomore guard and the second-leading

scorer that year. John Friedersdorf, who had led the team in scoring in Gunning's last two seasons, was back for his senior year. We also had Gary Thompson as a sophomore guard. Gary, who had played for me at East High, would go on to become my assistant at Wichita in the 1960s, and take my job when I left for Iowa in 1964.

We got people excited early. We lost our opener at Colorado, but in our first home game against Baylor, we won 93-59, establishing a school scoring record in our first appearance before the local fans.

That record didn't last long. The next night, we beat Creighton, 100-63. Although we weren't going to be very good that year, at least we gave people an inkling of what would come later: A fast-paced, captivating style. A couple of weeks after we set those records, we established a school record still on the books—120 field-goal attempts in a losing effort against Arizona.

Charlie Gill also came to us from East High. Unfortunately, he failed to make his grades following the first semester after starting for us. He could do some amazing things. He got a rebound once against Oklahoma A&M's 6'11" center, Bob Mattick, and with no other place to go, he squatted a little lower and dribbled right between Mattick's legs out into the open. That brought a little noise from the crowd.

The Long Road for Black Players

From the very beginning, going back to the days at East High, I had black players. Cleo Littleton was one. La Vannes Squires, who was the first black to play for Kansas University, was another. In fact, the year of our state championship, our nickname, the Blue Aces, was sometimes revised to Black Aces.

These were times of black athletes pioneering in athletics. Jackie Robinson and Larry Doby had broken the color barrier in baseball in the late 1940s. Yet there was still an uneven and arbitrary application of rules pertaining to black athletes that was obvious in the Missouri Valley Conference, which then stretched down to Tulsa, Oklahoma A&M and Houston.

During the 1951-1952 season, for instance, both of our games with Houston were scheduled in Wichita because no blacks had yet participated in football or basketball in the city of Houston. At

Stillwater, Oklahoma A&M had its own motel as part of its hotel-management program, so we could stay there. It seemed as though we fought the Civil War to give the black people their freedom, and as soon as we won the war, we said, "You're free, but there are restrictions."

I ran into prejudice my first year at East when we were sent to a regional tournament at Independence. We knew about the difficulty in finding a place that would serve blacks, so we made plans to drive over, drive back, and not spend the night. But we ran into a big sleet-snowstorm so we were isolated in Independence.

We had to stay over two extra days. We all got into a hotel all right, but finding a place to eat was another story. The only place I could find to serve them was the bus station.

"We'll feed them," I was told, "but they have to eat in the kitchen."

"Well," I said, "have you got a big kitchen?"

"Not particularly."

"Then it's sure as hell going to get crowded back there."

"What do you mean?

"If you put the two black players back there," I said, "then there's going to be 15 eating in the kitchen. Now look, it's dark, you've got booths, now you could put the two black players in the back booth and Frank Henkel and I will sit with them."

It finally worked out that way. We ate for three days in the bus cafeteria and that was the only way I could feed my black players. In fact, in Topeka, where the state tournament was played at that time, the only place you could find to serve blacks was a Chinese restaurant.

> **Cleo Littleton: "We went through a lot of hell because Ralph did believe in playing what he thought were the best athletes. Quite often, he was classified as a Globetrotter. My senior year at East, we used to start four black athletes.**
>
> **"One of my pet peeves was, I would not eat in the kitchen, no matter where. I would eat on the bus or in the car. In college, most of the time, I'd just stay on the bus and they'd bring out a hamburger for me.**

"I was the only black in the Missouri Valley Conference at the time. There was another one on the team, but he didn't travel. I was classified as the first black ever to play at Tulsa, the first black to play in Houston. In Houston, they would not allow me to play on campus. They rented a public gym and scheduled it for the Wichita games. In most instances, I'd have to stay with a black family.

"Fans were very, very negative about me playing. It continued throughout my career. They would always have some kind of racial remark.

"It was something I had gone through since high school. It was constant. Players would call you names, spit on you, kick you, knee you. I got kicked out of games at East quite a few times my sophomore and junior years. Then Ralph and Linwood Sexton, who was an All-American football player at Wichita, talked to me. Linwood, who's now a member of the Kansas Board of Regents, had gone through it, and he and Ralph said if I couldn't take it, I'd need to chuck it in right then. I'll say one thing for Ralph, he showed me a few tricks of the trade, how you can get even. A little elbow here, a knee there.

"I always considered Ralph an excellent coach. His strategy was beyond reproach. He taught me everything I know, but we just never got to be real close. I didn't think anybody could understand. I was fighting the battle on the floor out there. When I'd get out of the huddle, he'd always have some other suggestions, what I wasn't doing right. I'd say, 'But I've got another problem, this guy is kicking me.'"

Those were very tough times for blacks. When I recruited Dave Stallworth, our great All-American, to Wichita in the 1960s, he had no money, a couple of pairs of jeans, T-shirts, a pair of tennies and that was it. I was showing him around the campus, and we're walking along, and next thing you know, he's two steps back. I said, "Come on up here, what the hell are you doing?"

He said, "Well, Coach, I'm from Texas, and in Texas you walk two paces behind a white man."

"You're not in Texas now, you're in Wichita," I told him. "And don't ever forget it."

I remember another time, calling the YMCA in Dallas to try to find housing and meals on a trip. But they wouldn't allow blacks.

The first time we took Cleo to Houston was memorable. He fouled out, but he scored 33 points. I had a big old guy, must have weighed 300 pounds, sitting behind my bench. I have never heard a more foul-mouthed person, and he didn't like blacks. He was on Littleton the whole game. He called him "alligator bait"—you name it.

Cleo eventually fouled out and everybody was booing him. Suddenly, this same guy slung out his arms and said, "Shut up!"

And he was big enough to shut you up.

"You just watched the best damn basketball player you've ever seen in Houston," the man said. "Now clap!" The crowd offered a standing ovation for Cleo.

But it was hard to forget the difficulty those kids went through. Getting them a taxi to ride in was hard. Guy Lewis, the former Houston coach who was a good friend, used to always try to get me to come back and play Houston. "No way, Guy, no way." I'd tell him, "I remember Houston."

"Well, it's changed," he said.

"Yeah, I know. But I still remember and the only time I'm going to play in Houston is if I'm in a tournament and I have to."

I never did.

I first encountered the force of racial prejudice when I was a physical-training officer at Drew Field in Tampa. One of our projects was to prepare B-17 crews for England and Africa. We were their last stop. They not only had to complete their flight training, but all other requirements, including a swimming test. Well, we somehow lost track of a whole squadron so we were working against time to get them tested for swimming.

I talked to the commanding officer and said, "I'll tell you what, the best thing to do is to bring 'em in Wednesday afternoon.

That's the day blacks can swim and there's never more than three or four men who come swimming."

I went over and there were three blacks, sitting on the side of the pool, dangling their feet. I told them I had this squadron coming in 20 minutes for testing, and would they mind staying out of the pool until we finished? "No, lieutenant,"they said, "that's fine."

The squadron came in, and I had them all lined up.

"May I ask you a question, sir?" one lieutenant says. "Those blacks been in this pool?"

"Yes."

"Then I won't get in that water."

"What do you mean, you're not getting in the water? You've got to take the test."

"It doesn't make any difference. I'm not getting in any water that blacks have been in."

So I said, "All right, let me ask all of you a question. How many of you don't want to get in that pool?"

Seventeen hands went up.

I said, "Well, gentlemen, you've got to take this test, otherwise you don't get to take leave on Friday. This is your last week in the United States. You've got to take this test. Now how many of you won't get in that water?"

Ten hands went up.

"All right, I'll see that all of your leaves are cancelled. I'll meet you here at 8:00 Sunday morning. You're restricted to base until you take this test, and you cannot take it until 8:00 Sunday morning. Satisfactory?"

How ridiculous can you get? These people believed in a myth strongly enough that they would give up their final weekend in the United States because of it.

At any rate, I've always played blacks. In fact, I think one of the reasons I was hired at Oregon State in 1970 was that the school, like many at that time, had had racial problems in the late 1960s and I had a reputation for recruiting blacks.

Before we went to the state tournament that we won at East in 1951, I went to see my principal.

"Before we go, I want to ask you a question," I said, wanting to make sure I knew his feelings about the numbers of blacks playing. "Are we going to the state tournament to win it, or play politics?"

"We're going up to win," he said.

"That's all I want to hear," I said.

Great Coaches, Wild Games

Our second season produced a 16-11 record, the most wins at Wichita since, ironically, Gene Johnson's club went 18-5 in 1931. We won our first seven before the rigors of the Missouri Valley Conference caught up with us.

Only the veterans out there will remember it, but the Missouri Valley was simply a wicked basketball conference, widely considered the toughest in the country as well as being the oldest in the Midwest. Almost every stop was a potential loss. It was known as the Valley of Death.

It was a league that underwent much change, then and now. Schools came in and out because the football generally wasn't good enough. At one time, Kansas, Kansas State, Nebraska, Missouri, and Oklahoma were all members of the Missouri Valley. In the early 1920s, they withdrew and formed the Big Six with Iowa State. Later, Colorado was added to form the Big Seven, and still later, Oklahoma State made it the Big Eight.

When I came to Wichita University, the Missouri Valley Conference included Wichita, Detroit, Tulsa, Oklahoma A&M, St. Louis, and Houston. Several years into my Wichita tenure, it had new members in Drake, Bradley, North Texas State, and Cincinnati. It was Cincinnati that symbolized the toughness of the league, first with Oscar Robertson at the end of the 1950s, then with two national championships in 1961-1962 under Ed Jucker.

There were great coaches in the league, starting with Henry Iba, who had already won two national championships with Oklahoma A&M in 1945-1946. He would later coach three Olympic basketball teams. There was Eddie Hickey of St. Louis, a proponent of the fast-break and molder of excellent teams before the school de-emphasized basketball. Forddy Anderson had excellent teams at Drake, Bradley, and Michigan State.

There never was a lack of excitement. In my first season, we had an interesting situation involving a rule of that time. In fact,

its reinstatement is being discussed today. We were down by
seven to a very good St. Louis team at home with six minutes to
go, and came back within one, 64-63, when Paul Scheer was
fouled with 11 seconds left. He had one free throw available for
the tie, but we elected to take the ball out of bounds and go for the
victory, which you could do at that time. We didn't get off much
of a shot and lost. Actually, we had four such situations that year
— with a choice of possession or a free throw — and you might
think a person could bat .500 just by chance, but we went 0 for 4.

We had another wild time in our great 1954 season when
Scheer hit a 30-foot shot with two seconds to play to beat Iba's
Oklahoma A&M team, 67-66. It was the first time we had ever
won at Stillwater, and the students didn't take kindly to it. They
stuffed rags in the tailpipe of our bus, and it was blazing nicely
as we drove out.

I had a player named Don Laketa, who was graduating in
mid-season of 1955. His last game was going to be at Kiel
Auditorium in St. Louis, and unbeknownst to me, he had asked
Coach Hickey if he could have the game ball when it was over.
Eddie said that would be fine, but of course, I'd have to replace
it.

Well, we were beaten 73-71 in a cliff-hanger and after it was
over, the official put the ball down on the table and Don went
over to get it. A riot broke out. The fans saw Don take the ball,
and we ended up fighting our way out of that place. In the melee,
Cleo Littleton, who had no part in the affair, got decked. I had no
idea what had happened.

Then there was our victory at Cincinnati in 1964, the year
after Cincy had lost to Loyola of Chicago in the national championship game. The score was tied at 54, and Ernie Moore, our
senior guard, stole the ball with 45 seconds left to set up a final
shot for us. Stallworth took it and made it.

I watched the official, Floyd Magnusson, go to the scorer's
table, and motion that the basket was good. The officials signed
the book and they were gone. We were in the locker room when
10 minutes later, there was a rap on the door. It was Maggie,
saying, "I've got to talk to you, we've got a problem."

"What do you mean?"

"Coach, the timer says Stallworth's basket didn't count. He

says he reached for the gun, but it slipped out of his hand, so when he grabbed it and shot it, time had already expired."

"We don't have any problem," I said. "Go look at the rule book. The only thing that ends this game is the gun."

We hadn't beaten Cincinnati since it came into the league in 1958, and here we were, having to go do it again. We returned to the floor, and after Nate Bowman missed a couple of free throws for us, Stallworth followed the last one in and we won—again—59-58.

We were welcomed home by 10,000 fans at the airport. Later there was a delayed telecast of the game. My wife knew we had won the game, but when we got into this debacle at the end, I guess I put on quite a show on the bench for about 15 minutes. Jean said, "Settle down, Ralph. There's no reason to get upset. You're going to win, anyway."

In 1962 in a consolation game of the All-College Tournament at Oklahoma City, we found ourselves in a novel situation. We were down in numbers and had several players foul out, and for almost two minutes at the end of a game against Ladell Anderson's Utah State team, we had to go with four players. We actually held a one-point lead when we had to drop to four, and we managed to win by two. What struck me was that there were so many holes in a four-man zone that Utah State actually looked a bit confused as to which shot to look for. There was a feast of possibilities.

Honest Players

There were streaks, both good and bad. After Cincinnati dominated us during Robertson's great years, we got our share of revenge early in the 1960s. In 1962 we beat their national-championship team 52-51 on a jump shot with three seconds left by Lanny Van Eman, who later would coach under me at three schools. That broke Cincy's 27-game winning streak.

A year later Cincinnati had another streak going—37 games this time—but we pulled off the upset again on an incredible night by Stallworth. He scored 46 points in a 65-64 victory, hitting 14 of 22 from the field and 18 of 23 foul shots. He led us from six points down in the last three minutes.

Then there was Bradley. For some reason—probably that Bradley had good teams—we couldn't win for losing there. Thirteen times we went to Peoria in my Wichita tenure, 13 times we lost. Annually, I felt we played one of our best road games there, but something always went wrong. During my last year at Wichita, we were ahead by eight points fairly late in the game, and I thought, "By golly, we're finally going to win one here."

We were winding down. We had a great ball control team. Stallworth went down the lane wide open. There wasn't anybody within 10 feet of him—and he missed a layup. I don't remember any layup he missed like that, but he missed that one.   It destroyed our ball club. We lost 76-74 on a last-second shot.

Finally, during the 1982-1983 season at Oregon State, we took a team back and played in a four-team tournament at Bradley. By then, they were out of the old airplane hangar, Robertson Fieldhouse, and were playing in a new arena. Of all things, we got into the finals and won quite handily against Bradley. So now I'm a robust 2-13 in Peoria.

About Oscar Robertson. He used to drive our Wichita teams absolutely crazy. I think Oscar averaged about 45 or 46 points against us, and I was supposed to be a reasonably good defensive coach. Then finally, it clicked. After he beat us six times almost singlehandedly, I realized Oscar never wanted to guard the person that I wanted to guard him. Before that, I was making some poor kid defend Oscar by going from one side of the floor to the other to pick him up, an impossible assignment.

About that time, we changed our defensive philosophy to: Guard the person who's guarding you. You don't have time to run around looking for a person to guard. It fits in well with the principles of the 2-2-1, and it is a great method for keeping the opponent's fast-break under control. The break has to be slowed down before it has a chance to get started. During the great years of John Wooden at UCLA, we had consistent success slowing down the fast-break, simply by hindering that outlet pass — stopping the break at its inception.

In 1963, we beat both the participants in the NCAA championship game, Cincinnati and Loyola of Chicago. Ed Jucker, the Cincinnati coach, called me to ask how we had defensed Loyola's outstanding scorer, Jerry Harkness. I told him that we had actually done the job by using the simple rule of picking up the man who guards you.

In that national title game, Tom Thacker of Cincinnati would be guarded by Harkness, which benefited Cincy because Thacker was a great defensive player. Unfortunately, on a controversial play, Thacker drew his fourth foul.

Cincinnati had built a 15-point lead and Thacker had just shut Harkness off. But Jucker called timeout, switched defensive assignments and soon after, Harkness went on a scoring rampage. Loyola took the game into overtime and eventually won. I am convinced to this day that if Jucker had not changed those assignments, he would have been the first coach to win three consecutive NCAA championships.

Our first Wichita club had a freshman named Jim McNerney, and therein lies a story. I mentioned Jim Trimble, the athletic director before I arrived. He was from McKeesport, Pennsylvania.

Recruiting wasn't so structured then. Most of it took place the summer before freshmen enrolled. Trimble was reputed to rustle up a couple of station wagons, get one of his assistants and drive back to McKeesport, where they'd find out about any football player who had some talent and wasn't already set to go to a school. They'd load the bags in and be off to Wichita.

In my first year there, two brothers who were football players came in to see me. They were named George and Sneak Thomas. Sneak said, "Coach, we have a very good friend who is a good basketball player in McKeesport, Jim McNerney."

I was skeptical. Sneak was a pretty good basketball player himself. I told him this McNerney needed to be better than he was. He said he was. So I agreed to take McNerney sort of on the come. I promised to take a look at him, and if he was good enough to help, I'd give him a scholarship. So Jim came, enrolled, and after two weeks, I gave him a scholarship.

Well, through Jim, I became acquainted with the basketball coach at McKeesport, Neenie Campbell. He was one of the great athletes there in football, basketball, baseball, even boxing. He told me there were many good athletes in McKeesport. Neenie became a friend, and my recruiting of McKeesport the first five years consisted of picking up the telephone and calling Neenie: "Hey, Neenie, got anybody to recommend?"

At last count, through my Wichita State and Iowa tenures, I think I had 23 players from the McKeesport area. One time McNerney told me about a fellow named Ron Heller, also from McKeesport. He had never played basketball but Jim said he was a player. I called Neenie and he confirmed it. The kid was a good player, but Neenie said Ron was just too immature at that time.

I called Ron and said, "How about it?"

"Coach," he said, "I want to go to college, but like Neenie told you, I'm a little immature. So how about letting me come to school next year? I'd like to stay home and work for a year and just have a year to grow up."

That was fine with me. And in 1961, Heller, a 6' 7" forward, was the leading scorer on an 18-8 Wichita State team with 17 points a game.

Our best-known McKeesport product was Lanny Van Eman. Another football player from McKeesport came in to tell me that there was a player from home who had enrolled at North Carolina State but wasn't happy there. I couldn't do anything. I knew Everett Case, the North Carolina State coach, and told the football player Lanny would have to work it out with Everett.

Everett called me. "Ralph, take him," he said. "He's a good kid, he's just not happy."

Neenie recommended him, too. So Lanny came out, I paid his tuition, and got him a job until he became eligible. I had myself a three-year starter at guard, our leading scorer on the 1962 club, and an excellent assistant coach.

I was lucky. The kids from McKeesport were good, honest types who didn't try to sell me down the river for a friend. Neenie was the same way. I'd call him about some great players there, and he'd say, "Don't touch him. I don't want him playing for you."

This wouldn't be the last pipeline we would have. At Iowa, we pulled both John Johnson and Fred Brown out of Milwaukee. At Oregon State, we inherited Freddie Boyd out of Bakersfield. We later recruited Don Smith from there and that would ultimately lead to Lonnie Shelton.

For the most part, these weren't highly acclaimed players. Just players who could help us win championships.

Opening the Roundhouse

By 1954 we began to click. We opened at home by beating Fort Hays State and then took a trip to the Northwest, winning two of three in Seattle and Portland. A win at Portland signaled the start of a 14-game winning streak, and we knew we had something good going.

Setting Records in 1954

Cleo was an established star, averaging 18.2 points a game for us that year. The rest of the team wasn't abundantly talented, but the players knew their roles well and played together. By then we were very experienced. Cleo, Paul Scheer, and Gary Thompson were in their third years of starting, and Jim McNerney was a junior, starting for the second year. Certainly by today's standards we weren't very big. The center was a 6'6" fellow named Bob Hodgson. The substitutes were Don Laketa, Verlyn Anderson, Leo Carney, and Merv Carman. At 6'8", Carman was a 30-year-old master carpenter.

Hodgson was a great shooter. He came from a little old town of a few hundred called Weir, Kansas. Before he got to Wichita, he'd never had a haircut from a barber. Hodgson was a good player. He had a very bad ankle injury the following season, and didn't develop as he might have, but he still scored 17 points a game for us as a senior in 1956.

The 1954 team set 15 school records, although not all of them would attract notice today. For instance, we broke the field-goal percentage record with a mark of .395. Now, that kind of figure in a game usually equates to a loss. But at that time, for instance, McNerney's .443 shooting for 1953 was the school record. However, we did set a few lasting records, including wins in a season and points per game (80).

As the conference season began, we defeated Detroit in overtime, then followed with wins over Houston, Tulsa, and Detroit again. Eddie Hickey's St. Louis team broke the streak by beating us pretty soundly at St. Louis. In my first year at Wichita, Eddie, who had recruited me in high school, put his arm around me, and said, "Welcome to the clan, if there's anything I can do to help you, let me know."

I thanked him. Ed had come out to scout one of our games before we played at St. Louis that first year. So I went into St. Louis and picked up the papers that evening to see if there was anything about the ball game. There was a big story, with many quotes from Ed, saying in effect Wichita has a very young ball club, and they play basketball just the way they did in high school, so I really don't think we'll have a problem.

And he didn't. He beat us by 20 points or something like that. So one of my heroes went down the drain in a hurry, but I did learn from Ed. I learned from all of them, especially my first year. By the 1954 season, I was only 35.

Oklahoma A&M gave us our third, and final, loss of the regular season, but we were able to get that one back on their home court on Paul Scheer's long shot. That game created headaches for many people. In a scheduling quirk, it was our final conference game of the year. We still had non-league games against Emporia State and Oklahoma City. The win at Stillwater gave us a conference record of 8-2 and put A&M at 7-1 with two league games left to play. Had the Aggies lost one, we would have been forced to have a playoff, and that was the problem.

We had already accepted a bid to play in the National Invitation Tournament (NIT). The tournament picture was much different then. There was no announcement of NIT teams following the selection of the NCAA field as exists today. The reason was that the NIT was still considered a premier tournament, a plum as appealing as the NCAA. What is listed today as the first NCAA tournament, won by Oregon in 1939, was actually started by the National Coaches Association. The NCAA had nothing to do with it. The NCAA took over in 1940, the year of the Indiana-Kansas final, and has been running it ever since.

One of the reasons the Missouri Valley Conference grew to such respected status in basketball was that it gained favorable publicity by frequently sending teams to the NIT. During my tenure at Wichita, we went to the NIT three times, in 1954, 1962, and 1963.

In 1964, Walter Byers, the executive director of the NCAA, and his whole crew moved into Wichita for their spring meeting. The NCAA had convinced all other major conferences in basketball to send only their champion to the NCAA, while all other members of those conferences simply hung up their sneakers for the year. The Missouri Valley Conference (MVC) was the only league that did not go along with this policy, and the NCAA asked if we would join its side of the world. Fortunately, the MVC athletic directors and faculty representatives had common sense, and they said "no way."

The MVC's refusal to join the tide had a great impact for the next 15 years. It was during this period that the NCAA definitely was trying to relegate the NIT to the back seat as far as post-season play was concerned. As soon as the MVC balked at the NCAA proposal, other conferences immediately backed out of their agreements with the NCAA and started to send their runners-up to the NIT. After conferences were sending second-place teams to the NIT, the NCAA created a post-season tournament for those teams—the Collegiate Commissioners Association tournament—but it didn't fare well financially and was dropped. The move by the NCAA to quash the importance of the NIT continued when it began allowing a conference's second team into its tournament in 1975, and later, when it allowed for an unlimited number of teams from a conference. All along, the NCAA increased its field of teams in the tournament.

At any rate, in 1954, Oklahoma A&M solved the whole dilemma by winning its last two games, thus avoiding a playoff to decide who would go where. We were off to New York to play Bowling Green in the NIT.

The trip didn't last long, unfortunately. We trailed by seven at the half, and by 16 at the end of three quarters. In those days the college game had quarters. We made a big run at the end but lost to Bowling Green, 88-84. The crowd of 16,259 was the biggest the school had ever played in front of.

The primary culprit in our defeat was Al Bianchi, who had 29 points and would go on to a successful career in the National Basketball Association, as player, coach, and executive. Little did I know then that it wouldn't be the last of the post-season miseries my teams would experience.

Planning Weddings in 1955

The next year brought a 17-9 record, but it had its disappointments. We were supposed to have a pretty good ball club. In fact, many people were picking us to win the Valley. I'll always remember it as the year when matrimonial bliss interceded.

It began with Gary Thompson, my former player at East, and future assistant coach. Gary and his fiancée, Betty, had been sweethearts since they were about seven years old. Well, Gary's father and mother, and Gary's father's mother and father, had all been married on a particular date, and they wanted Gary and Betty to get married on that date.

I granted permission but suddenly we had five or six guys who wanted to get married, and having given permission to one, I ended up granting it to all of them. That year was a nightmare, and I think all the marriages had something to do with it. We just didn't play well. There was a divorce, an annulment, and a child was born to one of them. Wives were running to Jean for advice. There was enough concern among players with their marital situations that we just didn't perform.

That was also the year that introduced us to Phil Woolpert's fabulous future national champions from San Francisco with Bill Russell and K.C. Jones. As I said earlier, they beat us badly in the All-College Tournament. They got out to a 25-3 lead early and ended up beating us 94-75, their most points in history. It could have been worse; they led 53-23 at the half and played subs the last five minutes of each half.

Russell had 18 points and 22 rebounds — we only had 27 rebounds as a team — and I did something I never do. I went back the next afternoon, just to see them. I had to go watch this bunch again. I knew I was looking at a great basketball team.

Warming the Roundhouse

By 1956, we began a slide that we wouldn't reverse until the end of the decade. It wasn't a collapse by any means, but through the 1960 season, again we wouldn't win more than 15 games. Our best mark during that period was 15-11 in 1957. But the 1955-1956 season—during which we compiled a 14-12 record—had a bright side to it.

It was in December of 1955 that we moved into a brand new arena in Wichita, with a seating capacity of 10,235. We had been playing in the Forum, which seated about 4,400, and were ready for what would become known as The Roundhouse. It was circular and one of the palaces of its time. It cost $1.5 million, and was one of the best buildings for the money ever constructed. It's been a model for many of the round buildings constructed since then. One of them is Mackey Arena at Purdue although they put more seats in that building than we did in The Roundhouse.

It had all the accoutrements: Parking for 2,000 cars, the first steel-fabricated lamella roof in the nation, perfect lighting, and new office space for the athletic department. The building was erected in just 13 months.

Yet it was known by some as Miller's Folly. There were many people who thought we had no business in an arena that big, that we wouldn't be able to fill the place. For a few years they were right.

We had a waiting list for season tickets when we left the old Forum, but we had an excess of tickets to sell in the new building, and we didn't do it right off the bat. One reason was that they put all the plush seats on one side of the arena, which was a bad mistake. You could be 32 rows up in the plush seats, and it didn't take people long to figure out, "Why should I buy a season ticket when I can buy my games as I want them and sit lower on the other side?"

It's hard to argue with architects. So the attendance leveled off for awhile, but by the end of the 1950s, we were indeed selling out and continued to do so. As the years went on, and I went to Iowa and Oregon State, I'd issue this challenge to fans: Buy your tickets now because they won't always be available. And I was proven right. It didn't always happen right away, but it happened nonetheless. In the case of Wichita, it had always been a good basketball town.

When Wichita East was known as Wichita High School back in 1925, it won a state championship as well as the national high school tournament in Chicago. The old Wichita Henrys won an AAU title way back in the late 1920s, and they would put 4,000 people into the Forum to see them, so I was always confident about our ability to draw fans. One of the reasons I liked our system of execution was that it was exciting. You can't win all your games, but you do have to have people. You have to have interest.

Miller's Folly? The only folly was that for an additional $125,000 the roof could have been raised 25 feet, creating enough room for a balcony to bring the total capacity to 17,000 or 18,000. In the 1970s, this was a proposition still being entertained, and they checked into it and were told, yes, it could be done—for $13 million.

One of the reasons we slacked off to 14 wins that year was our schedule. It was murderous. Believe it or not, we played seven games against reigning conference champions. Besides the Missouri Valley schedule, with two games against defending champion Tulsa, we had to play Utah, UCLA, San Francisco, Southern Methodist, and Iowa — all league champs the year before. That might be unparalleled. Five of those league champions appeared at the Roundhouse, so the Wichita fans surely got their money's worth in that first season.

We christened the Roundhouse that year against a very good Utah team, coached by Jack Gardner. I had been trying to get Kansas to dedicate the fieldhouse but it just wouldn't budge. Dr. Allen had no problem with it, but the administration wouldn't hear of it. Neither Kansas nor Kansas State wanted anything to do with Wichita in my period.

I figured, at least I'm a graduate of Kansas, so I'll see. But Doc said he just couldn't get them to change their minds. So I went out and scheduled Utah to open the fieldhouse. Well, I didn't any more than do that than Doc called. He said he thought he'd convinced them to play us.

"That's great, Doc," I said. "But I've already scheduled the dedication with Jack Gardner."

"Maybe he'll change," Doc said.

"Doc, you know Jack Gardner isn't going to change anything."

Jack had coached at Kansas State, and he and Doc had been rivals for a long time. We reached a solution: Wichita opened the arena with a game against Jack's Utah team, and then we dedicated the building in our second appearance in it, against Kansas. It proved to be the only time my team ever played Kansas.

The opening of the building wasn't auspicious, at least from a performance point of view. We managed to hit seven of 41 shots in the first half and trailed 44-17. It didn't get much better in the second half, as we finished with 16 field goals in 72 attempts, a mere 22.2 percent. We lost 73-51. We didn't even sell out the building that night. There was an estimated turnout of 9,200.

It went better four nights later when we hosted Kansas. We still lost 56-55 in front of 10,000 people—the largest crowd ever for a basketball game at that time in Wichita—but played a much better game. After the game Doc Allen was quoted as saying, "Wichita built a wonderful fieldhouse here, but they made it too small. They built for the present instead of the future."

Probably not many people would have agreed with him, but he turned out to be right.

That game with Kansas was something of a milestone. It was the first time Wichita State had met KU since 1942, my senior season in college. Because of politics, the two schools wouldn't meet again until the NCAA tournament of 1981, when Wichita State came from behind and won in a regional semifinal game.

It was the old theory that still holds in many places: You had everything to lose and nothing to gain. Wichita State was clearly third on the totem pole in the state of Kansas. Kansas State wouldn't even participate in track meets with us. KSU won convincingly in basketball over Wichita the year before I arrived as head coach, and for all the time I was there, KSU would not schedule us.

Ultimately, Kansas State's football got so bad they were looking for somebody they might beat. That broke the ice, and they started playing football and basketball with Wichita. Shortly after I left Wichita in 1964, Ernie Barrett became athletic director at Kansas State, and he thought all this stuff was foolish so he deserves much of the credit for re-establishing the series. In 1970, after 19 years of divorce marked only by an NCAA tournament game in 1964, the two programs began playing basketball again.

I think that finally turned Kansas around, too. Their football program struggled before they started playing Wichita State in 1982. In recent years, the Kansas and Wichita State programs have been headed by coaches who had common ties to North Carolina, including Larry Brown, Roy Williams, and Eddie Fogler. Those factors, combined with the chance tournament basketball game in 1981, opened the door to a series between the two schools. They had actually gone 25 years without meeting in basketball.

Scheduling in the Late 1950s

In fact, we had an easier time then scheduling the national champions than we did our in-state rivals. After we had been embarrassed by Phil Woolpert's USF national champions in the 1954-1955 season, we were trying to schedule for the opening of the arena the next year.

"Can I talk you into coming back to Wichita for a game?" I asked Phil.

"Sure," he said. "You know, Ralph, you scheduled me when it was hard for us to get a schedule and I'll always remember that. I'll be very, very happy to come."

"Would $3,000 be all right for a guarantee?"

"Sure," Phil said.

That's how we lined up San Francisco to come to Wichita. We agreed to return the game in 1958. Can you imagine getting a national champion to come to your place today for a guarantee of only $3,000? By and large, I was the desperate one then, trying to build schedules, and I was able to get Nebraska, Iowa State, and other teams like them. At the same time, I understood why we couldn't get Kansas and Kansas State.

I've never had a hangup, however, about scheduling so-called lesser teams. At Oregon State, we had a yearly series with the University of Portland, home and away, and we took a few lumps doing it. At the same time, Oregon wouldn't schedule Portland.

It was during that 1955-1956 season when we opened the Roundhouse, that we played not only San Francisco, the defending national champions, but the Iowa team that would eventually face USF in the 1956 championship game.

We had an excellent game against USF and lost 75-65. Later, playing Iowa on the road, we were dismantled, 98-86. That was the Fabulous Five team coached by a good friend of mine, Bucky O'Connor.

Because of the common opponents, I got many questions about who I thought would win the national-title game. Although we had fared better against USF, in my heart I knew it had more potential and probably would win. And USF did, for the second successive year.

While we were having three straight 14-12 seasons from 1958-1960, we began putting the pieces in place for some better days. For one, the McKeesport connection had yielded Lanny Van Eman and Ron Heller. As I mentioned, Lanny was unhappy at North Carolina State and began calling schools that had recruited him out of high school.

Lanny Van Eman: "I think I took my final exam at NC State on maybe Thursday, and hitchhiked home on Friday. My brother met me out on the Pennsylvania Turnpike. There was two feet of snow on the ground.

"Saturday night I went to the Duke-West Virginia game. Both of them had recruited me. When I got home, I called Ralph. He said, 'Can you get an airplane out tomorrow?'

I told him I didn't have any money. My dad was a steelworker and had been out of work. I told Ralph I'd have to call him back. My dad said yes, he'd come up with the money. So I flew to Wichita on Monday and was going to class on Tuesday.

"I had to practice with the freshmen. Three or four days after I got there, I got in a fight with

one of the scholarship players, and it didn't sit
very well. Ralph called me in. They called him
The Ripper. You have no idea how demanding
and tough he was. He made it very clear to me his
better judgment was to send me home, but he'd
give me one more chance."

There were some rocky moments late in the decade of the
1950s. Those three 14-12 seasons didn't sit well with many
people. One influential booster felt I should be moving on, and
there were some other fans who felt the same way. One colum-
nist, Joe Gilmartin, was also critical, but I had no problem with
my president or with the school.

Building for Better Days

We took a difficult 72-70 defeat at home against Bradley in
1959, one in which we blew a lead, and that brought a lot of
people down on me. That loss was topped by another one the
next season, also at home, also against Bradley. It was nothing
short of bizarre. We had lost a pretty good lead and were trailing
by one point inside the final minute, 71-70. Foul trouble was
hurting us, and I had to substitute a 6' 3" sophomore named John
Allen, another product of McKeesport.

I called timeout and said, "Now look. They're going to sit in
a zone defense. Let them sit. But with 15 seconds to go, I want the
ball passed to Lanny at the point, and he will create the action."

Well, they threw the ball over to this kid, John Allen. He held
the ball, put it under his arm. He was still standing there with 15
seconds left. He was close to my bench, and everybody was
screaming at him. But he didn't throw the ball to Lanny. Finally,
with about one or two seconds left, he cast the ball high into the
air. Everybody was in shock. He thought we were ahead, not
behind.

Lanny Van Eman: "He dribbled the game
out, threw the ball into the air, and ran into the
dressing room. Ralph came in screaming. Ralph
never forgave John Allen. He eliminated him

from the team the following year. What clouded the whole thing was, there was an awful lot of talk in Wichita and Peoria that the game could have been fixed. Bradley had been through a lot during the point-shaving scandal earlier.

"As a teammate, I knew better. John was awfully religious. Something like that would have been the furthest thing from his thinking."

So I had my detractors. There were people who thought it was my fault for not getting across to Allen that we had needed to score to win. After that first Bradley loss, the whole thing became focused, when one night, I found an effigy of myself hanging from a telephone pole on campus. Not only that, my house was egged while Jean and I were gone, and my daughter, Susan, was babysitting our two youngest children. I didn't like it very much.

Lanny Van Eman: "We were having a post-game meal one night at Brown's Grill. Brownie was Ralph's best friend. Tommy Reilly, another McKeesport player, was with me. Somebody said Ralph's been hung in effigy. So we drove out to see it.

"We climbed up, took it down, and started to take it back to the dormitory. But we got another sign, like the back of one of those schedule posters, and put Joe Gilmartin's name on it. So we went back two hours later and hung it up again, and the next morning, there it was, hanging there with Joe Gilmartin's name on it."

We rode out the tough times. You learn to develop a thick skin in this business. Although people might not have realized it then, better days were ahead.

7

Putting the Pieces Together

The rough times did not last much longer.

Along with McKeesport, we began tapping into another pipeline, this one in Texas. The first catch was Johnny Gales, a 6'5" forward from Fort Worth. I knew coaches at Southern Methodist University and Texas Christian University, so I called them up and told them we hadn't had a chance to see John play. Well, they said, if he's black, we don't know anything about him.

These schools still weren't recruiting blacks.

Tapping the Texas Pipeline

It was very hard to find out anything about Johnny Gales, but we gambled on him. He started two years and contributed heavily to our program. Today John is a high school coach in Fort Worth whose team won a state championship two years ago, and his brother, Jimmy, is head coach at North Texas State.

We had it pretty easy in Texas because nobody was using black athletes. Our next player from that area was a real coup. I had a good friend, Linwood Sexton, who had been an All-American in football for Wichita. He had a relative in Amarillo, and through their correspondence, we heard about a 6'10" player there named Gene Wiley.

I went down there to see him and talk to his high school principal. It turned out, he had dropped out of school on two different occasions as a youngster. The reason he graduated, so to speak, from athletics, was that he got too old to play in Texas.

"You really think he could make it in college?" I asked the principal.

"Yes, if he wants to," he said. "Gene is an intelligent young man, but he has a problem. He's dropped out of school two times, his mother and grandmother have nothing. His major interest is art, and we don't even have an art class to offer him. I think if he were to go to a school where he could get some art, he'd prove to be a good student."

"Suppose it's possible for him to come to Wichita and complete his high school education?"

"It's entirely possible," the principal said, "but in order to do this, he's going to have to work. He's got a full year to go."

Gene came to Wichita and worked four to eight hours on the swing shift, paid all of his expenses, and took a few art classes. In his year at East High School, he was better than a B student in English and other subjects. It proved to us he was just one of those kids who had never had a chance. He had the tools.

Gene was a classy young man. Next to Bill Russell and Wilt Chamberlain, he was probably the best shot-blocker in America at that time. He ended up being a second-round draft choice of the Lakers, and was our first player to make the pro ranks.

I probably made a big mistake with Gene because he only played one year of basketball before Wichita and he didn't know very much. I told him I didn't want him to worry about offense. I wanted him for defense and rebounding, and he learned those trades well. In 1962 when we upset Bradley, which was seventh-ranked at the time, Gene had 26 rebounds. Then there was that game in Oklahoma City against Utah State, when we finished with four players on the floor because of foul trouble. We played kind of a diamond zone with Gene in the middle.

There were so many holes in that defense. But Utah State would figure, we can get closer than this, and when the shot would go up, Gene would block it. He'd not only block it, he'd catch it in mid-air. He was a great defensive player. However, by de-emphasizing his offense I had made a big mistake. I thought his offense would take care of itself. He rarely shot, but he was a good shooter. He started for us for three years and never averaged more than 13 points a game.

The minute he graduated, he signed a contract with the Lakers and bought his mother a house in Wichita—typical of

Gene. He's an artist today, works with Arco in Los Angeles. He retired from basketball only when his knees fell apart.

> **Jim Murray, *Los Angeles Times*, 1963:** **"(Gene) is so self-conscious and shy that he shambles on the court almost apologetically. He has never been known to lose his temper. He has spent most of his life in hiding. He is an oil painter by predilection, an athlete by accident, and if he could make $13,000 a year on canvas, you would never find him on backboards.**
>
> **"Wichita took an interest in his education, transferring him to East High School for his senior year, where they solicitously suggested he concentrate on studies and forego basketball for a year. Gene thought it was the most thoughtful gesture he had ever seen. And it was. If he had played his last year, there wouldn't have been enough money in Wichita to match the offers he would have gotten elsewhere.**
>
> **"He jumps so high on the court, he gets almost more goal-tending calls than the rest of the league put together. He plays the game with the silent stare of a man who has just seen two ghosts."**

By 1960, Gales and Ron Heller were seniors and Wiley was a junior, and we made a couple of scores in Texas that would put us back in the limelight. I had a friend who worked in the aircraft business in Fort Worth. He was from Wichita, had worked there for Boeing at one time, and he was always trying to send me players from Texas. In 1960 he was in Boston, and he boarded an airplane to come back to Dallas. By chance, there happened to be a group of Olympic athletes returning to Dallas, among them the sprinter Stonewall Johnson, who had been fifth in the 200 meters in Rome. My friend chatted with them and naturally got around to talking about basketball.

"I could tell you where the best basketball player in Texas is,"

Stonewall Johnson said. "He's at Madison High and his name is Dave Stallworth."

So Rusty called me to recount the conversation with Johnson and I said, "Go take a look, call me back and tell me what you think of Stallworth. If you think he's worth us coming down, we'll send my brother Dick down."

Rusty called back in early December.

"Ralph," he said, "he is the best basketball player I've ever seen in high school. I've been trying to get you a basketball player for 10 years, and I've been looking in the wrong gymnasiums."

I sent Dick down, and he came back.

"What do you think?" I asked.

"Ralph," he said, "you've never had anybody as good as he is."

It was one of the easiest recruiting jobs I ever had. Until Oklahoma State came in late, we were the only four-year school to offer Dave Stallworth a scholarship. He was another mid-semester graduate. That wasn't all. The game Dick saw Stallworth play in was against a team from Fort Worth.

"They had a player named Bowman, Nate Bowman," Dick said. "He's 6'10" to 6'11", just like Wiley. Doesn't know a thing about basketball, but he gets up and down the floor pretty well."

We found out that Nate had broken his wrist early in his career so his mother said, that's it, your career is over. He finally persuaded her to let him come out as a senior, and it was early in the year we saw him.

So I called Nate Bowman. "Nate, you know Dave Stallworth, don't you?"

"Sure, Coach, I know Dave."

"How'd you like to play basketball with Dave the next four years?"

"Oh, that would be great."

"Do you know I have him here at Wichita?"

"No, I didn't. He's at Wichita?"

"I just thought you might like to play with him."

"I sure would, Coach. I sure would."

We played at North Texas State in our last game of the 1960-1961 season, and Nate asked me if he could bring his family over to meet me. I said sure. Well, it ended up costing me 24 tickets for his family. Fortunately, my team didn't need any.

He strode into the gym, all 6'10", dressed to the hilt, and walked right past the North Texas bench to ours, where we all shook hands. The North Texas coaches did not even know who he was or where he was from. They tried to get into the act, but as far as Nate was concerned, there was only one place he was going to school.

Stallworth was simply a superlative player. At 6'7", he could play either guard or forward, although we used him primarily at forward. After he was in Wichita a while, I told people he had the potential to rival the talents of Oscar Robertson, and I may not have been far off. Once again, we were in the days of freshman ineligibility. In three years, he had 20 games of scoring 30 points or more for us. He had 46 when we beat Cincinnati 65-64 in 1963. He had 23 rebounds when we beat Creighton in the NCAA playoffs in 1964.

Bowman arrived a semester later. Dick was right. He sure didn't know anything about basketball. He could run up and down, but he tested your patience. I think it was the fifth or sixth day of running figure-eight drills before he caught more than one or two balls. It was two weeks before he caught one and made a good pass. I always remember the first time he caught the ball and tried to pass it across the court on the run. The ball went over the receiver's head by 15 feet, clear up into the bleachers.

Yet, when he was a junior, he made one of the most beautiful plays I've ever seen. Somebody made a mistake and threw him the ball in the middle of the court on a fast-break. He was running full-steam and some little guard decides he'll take a charge. We threw Nate the ball, he caught it, passed off, side-stepped this guard, and went right on down the court. If you'd been with him the first six months, you wouldn't have dreamed he'd be able to do that.

Nate started for us for three years, and like Dave Stallworth, ended up being a first-round draft choice in the NBA. They played with the New York Knicks and became NBA champions together.

Tragically, Nate's life was short. He was making a living doing commercials some years back. He had just walked out of a recording studio, said goodbye to the secretary, turned, and started toward the door. He never made it. Nate Bowman had a massive heart attack and died at 40.

Unfortunately, I didn't maximize my resources when Stallworth and Bowman arrived. Stallworth, as I said, was one of those mid-semester graduates, and so he became eligible mid-way through the 1961-1962 season. I had the option of playing him right away, or waiting until the 1962-1963 season, when he would have been a sophomore in eligibility. I chose to have him eligible in mid-season of 1961-1962. Maybe it was a remote possibility, but I thought with Stallworth, we had a good chance to beat out Cincinnati for the conference title. We were right with them at the time.

It was one of the bigger mistakes I've made in coaching. Dave really helped us, averaging 19.8 points a game that season. Unfortunately, Gene Wiley tore up his ankle. We lost four of our final six games, finished 18-9, including a loss to Dayton in the NIT. Cincinnati won the title. Maybe Cincy would have made me look foolish anyway because that was the team that beat Ohio State for the second straight season in the national championship game.

My decision to play Dave immediately would have a profound effect on Wichita fortunes, as we would see.

Missing Some Talent

In 1961 we attracted a person to Wichita who would be very important to me for many years. My first recruiting class at Wichita had included Verlyn Anderson, a 6'2" guard from McPherson, Kansas. He would later go on to assist Gary Thompson at Wichita when I left the program. Well, the state tournament happened to be in the Roundhouse in 1961, and Andy had given me the names of two players from McPherson that he thought could play for me. All I had to do was walk out of my office, but I didn't bother to pick up a program.

McPherson won, and after the game, Verlyn came up and asked, "What do you think, Coach?"

"The only one I'm interested in," I told him, "is that dark-haired one."

"But that's not one of the better players."

"The only kid I'm interested in," I insisted, "is the dark-haired one. What's his name?"

"That's Dave Leach."

"I'll give Dave Leach a scholarship, but not the other two."

Fortunately, I've had a long association with both Verlyn and Dave. Verlyn was a regional supervisor for the Coleman Company, and lived in the Northwest for years. Dave, of course, started for two years at Wichita and coached with me for ten years at Oregon State.

Dave was a little slow afoot, but he was a very intelligent player and a great shooter. He was such a great corner shooter that in the Roundhouse, they used to call his left corner "Leach's Corner." We played one night at Minnesota in 1963, and, of course, we had Stallworth and Bowman. They were supposed to be our keys, so Minnesota just left Dave alone in the corner by himself. He had 22 points at halftime and we won.

Dave was from a family that didn't have much money so he was going to college in order to help out financially. We set him up at a bank and they loved him. He moved from a bottom teller to a top teller in one summer and they thought he had a great future in banking.

By Dave's senior year, I was at Iowa. I went down to see Wichita play Drake at Des Moines, and Dave asked if he could talk to me after the game.

"Coach," he said, "I don't think I want to go into the bank business. I think I want to be a coach."

"Dave," I said, "you can't even get a job. You're not in education."

But he was a very smart kid. He received an NCAA scholarship, took an extra year and got his teaching credentials. He was an assistant coach at North High School in Wichita, then became head coach at Southeast High, where he won two state championships. Later, he went on to Burlington Junior College in Iowa, the school that would enroll a couple of our Iowa standouts, Sam Williams and Fred Brown.

In 1970, one year after he'd been at Burlington, I decided to move to Oregon State. Lanny Van Eman, one of my assistants, got the head-coaching job at Arkansas. Dick Schultz succeeded me at Iowa. So I called Dave.

"I've got a proposition, Dave," I told him. "I need to hire an assistant coach to go with me to Oregon State and just wanted to know if you'd like to consider."

"Yes," Dave said. "I've already considered it."

"You don't have to make a decision now. Think it over."

"We've already thought it over. I'll go with you."

Dave was with me ten years, then got the head coaching job at Boise State. They gave him only three years there, and he entered the field he was studying almost 20 years prior. He's now at Merrill Lynch in Boise. Still handles all my finances.

We began the 1963-1964 season by winning six of our first eight, the sixth a victory at Minneapolis. The night before was the easiest night I ever had on the road. It was so cold outside, and the kids from Texas were used to warm weather. Nobody wanted to go out. It was a memorable, and not altogether pleasant, trip. We went on to Columbus and lost to Ohio State, and there, our bus gave out so the players all got out and pushed it. Then the heaters on our DC-3 went belly-up on the way back to Wichita, and we had the choice of landing for repairs, or simply going on. We went on with the kids huddled under blankets.

> **Dave Leach: "In Columbus, we stayed in this old hotel, the kind that had elevators with people running them. There was a beautiful girl running this elevator and Nate Bowman fell in love with her. He rode the thing up and down, all night long. Well, the next night, Gary Bradds of Ohio State is just eating Nate alive and Ralph calls timeout. He grabs Bowman by the cheek and says, 'You're cute. Sit down.'**
>
> **To this day, I don't know if he knew Nate had been occupied all evening."**

Making the NCAA

With Stallworth averaging 26.5 points a game in the 1963-1964 season, we went 23-6, beat Drake in a playoff game, and made the NCAA tournament for the first time in my career. We had the benefit of the regional being played at Wichita, but it only helped so much.

We beat Creighton in the first game there, 84-68, but lost the next night to Kansas State, 94-86. One of our starters during the season, Ernie Moore, a guard, had averaged 17.4 points a game for us, second only to Stallworth. He had been academically ineligible earlier in his career, so on a technicality, he could only play through the conference season and no longer. When it came to the NCAAs, he was out. Had we had Ernie, there's no question in my mind, we would have won.

> **Dave Leach: "After that season, we had a huge banquet. Everybody's all enthusiastic, the whole works. Ralph stood up, and the first thing out of his mouth was, 'Where were you people when those guys egged my house back in 1959?'**

1964-1965 Eligibility Problems

Eligibility again was a choice topic for Wichita in 1964-1965. With Stallworth, Bowman and Leach as seniors, and a 6' 2" guard named Kelly Pete who averaged 17 points a game, Wichita had an excellent team, going 21-9. However, my decision on Stallworth in the 1961-1962 season proved to be costly. Halfway through the 1964-1965 season, he had finished his eligibility. Then Wichita lost Nate Bowman to low grades.

Somehow, without Dave and Nate, that club struggled all the way to Portland for the Final Four. It lost to the eventual national champ, UCLA, and then to Bill Bradley's fabulous 58-point night for Princeton in the consolation game.

But the club did a remarkable job—for the new coach, Gary Thompson. By this time, I was on my way to Iowa.

Part III
Coaching at Iowa

8

On to Iowa

Early in February of 1964, I got a call from Forest Evashevski, the athletic director at Iowa. Sharm Scheuerman, who had played on the 1955-1956 Fabulous Five Iowa team, had resigned as coach after six years. Evy asked if I had any interest in coming to Iowa, and the answer was yes. I learned later that Doug Mills, the Illinois athletic director, previously an outstanding basketball coach, had recommended me.

We had a very good season going at Wichita, and I wanted to wait until that was completed so we agreed to suspend any talks until then. Our season ended with the defeat to Kansas State, and Jean and I went to the Final Four at Kansas City without having heard anything more from Evy.

Welcome to the Big Ten

In the meantime, something else of interest was taking place. Dick Harp, successor to Dr. Allen at Kansas—and a former teammate of mine—had resigned as the head coach at KU. Wade Stinson, the athletic director at Kansas, paid Jean and me a visit during the Final Four. He said that he and the athletic board members at KU would like to hire me as the new basketball coach, but a mandate from the state legislature prevented it.

It seems that Wichita University was accepted as a member of the state system of higher education in 1963, but it would not take effect until the 1964-1965 school year. A rider attached to the bill stipulated that from July 1, 1963 until June 30, 1964, there would be no exchange of personnel—including coaches—between Kansas, Kansas State and Wichita University.

Back to Evy. Our February conversation was, of course, to have been a secret, but it leaked out. On our first evening in Kansas City for the Final Four, Jean and I ran into Branch McCracken, the Indiana coach, and Forddy Anderson, coach at Michigan State.

"Welcome to the Big Ten," McCracken said.

"You'll enjoy working in the Big Ten," Anderson added.

"Thanks," I said, "but I haven't yet talked to Evy."

The next morning, several members of the media approached me in the hotel lobby. "What's the story?" they asked. "We hear you're going to Iowa."

"Look, gentlemen," I said. "I haven't talked to Evy since early February, so all you have is a rumor."

Right then, Jean walked up and passed me a note from the front desk. After the press had dispersed, I read it: "Call Mr. Evashevski at the Continental Hotel."

I went to the Continental, where Evy and the president of the Iowa athletic board awaited. Evy was brief and straightforward. "We want you to be the next basketball coach at Iowa," he said, adding that he would like to have Jean and me visit the campus. I agreed to a visit.

We had planned to drive to Iowa City, but a typical Midwestern sleet and ice storm hit the area so we drove from Wichita to Kansas City and then took the train from there to Iowa City. On the way to Kansas City, we stopped in Topeka and called to thank Brice Durbin for recommending me for the Kansas job — and he asked us to stop in Lawrence and talk to Mitt Allen. Mitt was the son of Dr. Allen and one of the people who had been pushing my candidacy for the Kansas position. Brice also informed me that the Kansas State Patrol had been put on the lookout for my car so I would get the message to call Mitt. We were never stopped, however. I called Mitt and he said he didn't think the door was closed yet for me at Kansas, but I told Mitt to forget it. I thought it was a dead issue; my future was in Iowa.

We had a good visit in Iowa City. I liked Evy's style. He said he knew football but knew very little about basketball, and would leave the program totally in my hands, which he did for all of my six years at Iowa. I accepted the job at $16,500 a year, which, believe it or not, made me the highest paid coach in the Big Ten. Just before we left, I got another call from Brice, informing me that Ted Owens had just been named coach at Kansas.

I was relieved. It would have been very difficult to have to make a choice between Kansas and Iowa. Kansas was a great school, had an outstanding basketball reputation, and, of course, the lure of returning to one's alma mater is magnetic. Had I accepted that position, I'd have probably still been there when I retired.

Perhaps a passage from a cover story Frank Deford of *Sports Illustrated* did on our program in early 1966 will help to explain our move to Iowa:

> **"I was 45 when the Iowa offer came," he quoted me. "It was a watershed year. I had been around basketball for 20 years, and I had about 20 years ahead of me. A man at that point needs a new challenge. If not, you can get too secure— and pretty soon, things pass you by."**

Teaching the Fast-Break

I made my usual challenge about buying tickets early, because they wouldn't always be available. However, there was much initial skepticism about our style.

The popular question was, "Well, Coach, what style of basketball will you use this year? Obviously, you won't be able to fast-break and use pressure defense with the personnel you inherited."

"It's easier to teach young pups new tricks," I responded, "than to change the habits of an older dog. I'm older than the players, so we'll teach them some new tricks."

Our players responded beautifully, although it wasn't an immediate transition. In fact, the first two weeks of practice were beyond belief.

Lanny Van Eman came into my office and said, "Ralph, you know I'm a believer, but do you really think we can make a pressure team out of this group?"

We didn't start very auspiciously, beating South Dakota handily but losing to Kentucky and Evansville. We averaged 31 turnovers in those three losses. Yet this was the same group that would score 111 points, a school record, in beating Michigan State in January. Later that month at Chicago Stadium, it would knock off that year's national champion, UCLA, 87-82, when that team was top-ranked. I got carried off the floor on my players' shoulders.

That put me 3-0 against John Wooden. But he'd get even soon enough.

When I got the job, I had a conversation with my good friend Arthur Morse, the attorney in Chicago who promoted events at Chicago Stadium. Arthur wanted us to sign a five-year contract to play UCLA at the stadium, the first game to be in the coming season.

"Arthur, that's ridiculous," I said. "I know they've already recruited a fellow named Alcindor."

I said I'd play them this year — the year before Lew Alcindor arrived as a varsity player — under one condition. We were going to have to go play in the Los Angeles Classic, but I didn't want to be on the same side of the bracket as UCLA. We got it worked out.

We played at Los Angeles, winning two out of three and beating Minnesota by two points. The kids had lost to Minnesota three straight times so that gave them a little confidence and they started to roll.

By watching that tournament, and not having to worry about playing UCLA, we were able to get a read on Gail Goodrich, the guard, who would be the big scorer when UCLA beat Michigan for the NCAA championship that year. In Chicago, we held Goodrich down and won the game, in the midst of a stretch in which we won eight of ten games. We would finish fifth in the Big Ten at 8-6.

Our last game that year, at Minnesota, gave me another lesson in faulty officiating. There, we ran into one more textbook case of: What ends the game, the timekeeper's intention to end it, or the horn?

It had happened in my last year at Wichita and it also happened at Minneapolis against Iowa's big rival. We were in a tie game and Lou Hudson, the Minnesota great, took a last-second shot. He jumped into my defensive player, the whistle blew and he missed the basket. The official called charging. The kid going to the free-throw line for us was a great shooter. I jumped up onto that raised floor at Minnesota and caught the official coming down.

"Let me understand this," I said. "Hudson's fouled us. My kid has a one-and-one and there's no time on the clock."

"That's right," he says.

He took my free-throw shooter to the line. There was nobody else there, just the two of them. He handed my player the ball, and the horn went off. The other official came over and grabbed the ball and says, "Let me explain the situation. The timekeeper says he missed the horn on the first try."

"If anybody knows this rule," I said, "it's me. I made national publicity last year at Cincinnati for the same thing. It doesn't make any difference what happened to the timekeeper or if he missed that horn. The rulebook says the horn ends the contest."

Well, you never win an argument. We went into overtime in that one and lost 85-84.

I got introduced to radio broadcasting, Iowa style, that year. Most universities let their radio rights out for bid, and the highest bidder carries the games. Iowa contracted with each station individually, so there were 26 to 30 stations carrying Iowa football.

My first year there, I think I had four or five post-game radio shows, all on different stations. The game would get over, and maybe an hour and a half later, I could go home. They were perfectly happy to go down the line in order, but they all had their own show.

After a year of that, I said this is foolish, so I proposed a new format. We'd get all the stations together, they could ask questions in order, and we might even bring in one newspaperman to take part. Everybody bought it except WHO in Des Moines. They decided to have me do my own pre-game show. I tried to tell them the post-game show would make a lot more sense, but they wanted a pre-game show anyway. So I did. But we consolidated all those post-game shows, much to my relief. All of them paid me exactly the same money I had been making on individual shows.

My First Iowa Team

We finished 14-10 that first year, and it was a delightful bunch of kids. I've probably never had a greater group of future achievers. Fred Riddle became a dentist. Denny Pauling is a vice president at PepsiCo. Mike Denoma is a vice president at 3M. Gary Olson became a medical doctor. George Peeples played pro basketball and is now an oral surgeon in Los Angeles. Lew Perkins became athletic director at Wichita State, and then at Maryland.

Then there was our captain, Jimmy Rodgers, until recently the head coach of the Boston Celtics. At the end of his junior year, 1964, Jimmy had already been admitted to dental school. But he came to me and said, "I'd like to be a coach."

Well, I'd already heard this before from Dave Leach. I told him he should finish up his degree and come back in the spring and see if he'd had a change of heart.

He hadn't. Jimmy was hired as a graduate assistant by Bill Fitch, then head coach at University of North Dakota. Fitch went to Bowling Green after a couple of years and Jimmy headed the North Dakota program. Then, the year I came to Oregon State, Lanny got the head-coaching job at Arkansas, and Jimmy went with him for one year. By then, Fitch had moved on to the Cleveland Cavaliers, and he was able to offer Jimmy a substantial raise and entry into the pro ranks. Jimmy accepted.

That first Iowa team was led in scoring at 21.1 by Chris Pervall, a 6'3" transfer from Coffeyville, Kansas, Junior College. Chris became the forerunner to something of a tradition during my Iowa years: A select group of junior college players would be one of the keys to our success.

George Peeples, whom we inherited as a junior, was second in scoring at 17 points a game, and our leading rebounder. He was also an example of how we were still benefiting from other schools' reluctance to integrate.

Both Pervall and Peeples nearly ended up at Tulsa. Pervall signed a Missouri Valley Conference letter of intent with Tulsa—back in the days when there were such things—but we got him on the national letter. Peeples' case was more interesting. A 6'8" product of Ecorse, Michigan, Peeples sent back a form indicating interest in the school. Then he got back a post card saying Tulsa hadn't been aware he was a black player. It encouraged him to go to a junior college for two years in hopes the situation would change.

Peeples also encountered a bizarre situation at Davidson College in North Carolina. He was to take a recruiting visit there, got off the plane, and was spotted by officials from the school, who hadn't realized he was black. They sent him back to Michigan on the next plane.

Coaching a Seasoned Team

We headed into the 1965-1966 season with high expectations. It was hard not to be eager. We returned eight of our top nine players and the kids had had a year under our system with substantial success the first season. I went in believing we could contend for the Big Ten title. And we did.

We started terrifically. We won our opener against Pepperdine, 111-50, matching the school record for points we had set the year before. The pressure concept kicked in even sooner than normal in that one. We got off to a 32-2 lead and led 66-20 at halftime.

On the road, we beat Evansville, the defending national college division champion. That broke a 35-game winning streak that spanned three seasons. We kept winning through December. We took six more wins and climbed to ninth in the national polls. Then, through a series of upsets of teams ranked above us, we found ourselves rated fourth in the nation. I had a feeling we were overrated, and I would soon get a rude awakening.

Playing in the finals of the Sun Bowl at El Paso, we were clobbered 86-68 by little-known and unranked Texas Western. The world would know about that club—with Willie Cager, Willie Worsley, Nevil Shed, David Lattin—in due time. Don Haskins, the head coach, started five black players in the national championship game that season and they shocked Kentucky and the world with a victory.

Our problem in the Big Ten that year was that we couldn't seem to win on the road. We went unbeaten at home, but not until

February 19, at Ohio State, did we get a victory on the road. I was quoted that I didn't think the early No. 4 ranking had been good for us, insofar as it wasn't really earned. Texas Western had beaten us so soundly, holding us without a field goal for the first 10 minutes of the game, that our confidence got shaken.

In February, we lost our third-leading scorer and second-leading rebounder to academic ineligibility, a 6'4" forward from Chicago, Gerry Jones. His place in the line-up was taken by Ben McGilmer, a 6'7" mid-year high school graduate who had played just one and a half years of basketball. He was the last of several players recommended to me by Fred Snowden, then a high school coach in Detroit, who went on to become an assistant at Michigan and later the head coach at Arizona.

Ben made one of the most fantastic plays I've ever seen in basketball. He rebounded a shot, threw the outlet pass, and made a slam-dunk on the fast-break at the other end. The ball was never dribbled once. Now that's speed. Ben McGilmer would leave school after 1966 to enter the Army, but would return after his hitch to play on our most memorable team at Iowa.

Our road troubles kept us from doing better than a second straight 8-6 year in the Big Ten, but at least it was good for third place this time. Pervall and Peoples were the leading scorers in a 17-7 season, but we gave our most valuable player award to a forward who was only 6'4" and averaged just 7.8 points a game for us—Denny Pauling, from the little town of Paullina, Iowa.

Playing for the Big Ten Title

The year 1966-1967 found us contending for the Big Ten title, but coming up short once more. Considering that we had lost Pervall, Peeples, Pauling, and another senior, Gary Olson, it was a very good year.

We won eight of our first ten, including an upset of Cincinnati at Chicago, 78-69, when Cincy was seventh-ranked and unbeaten. It seemed as though once the Oscar Robertson era passed, we had success with that team. Our club was bolstered by another very good junior college player, Sam Williams. Sam was a player. He was about 6'3" and a big-time scorer out of Detroit. Williams would go on to become a first-round draft choice by the Milwaukee Bucks.

The interesting angle on Sam was that he didn't get to college right out of high school. He spent two years hauling meat in a cold-storage plant in Detroit. He had a persistent cold from that job one summer and decided there had to be something better. So he went to Burlington Junior College in Iowa and had several good scholarship offers, but we were nearby. He saw us play a couple of times and decided he liked our style. When I'd talk about Sam, I always referred to his decision to come out of the deep freeze.

The game before the victory over Cincinnati, we played Wichita State at Iowa City. Gary Thompson, whom I had been associated with for 14 years—first as coach at East High when he played, and then when he was my assistant at Wichita—called me and said he wanted to schedule a home game.

"Gary," I said, "this is a no-win proposition for both you and me. I don't think it's wise."

Well, he talked me into it, anyway. We ended up hosting Wichita in December of 1966 and beating them, 94-76. Some Wichita rooter hoisted a big sign in that section that said RALPH MILLER: WICHITA LOVES YA BUT NOT TONIGHT. Wichita did get its pound of flesh, however. Two years later, I made my first pilgrimage back to the city and took a 93-88 loss. So we were even.

I never really did like the idea of returning to an old haunt. Nobody wins in that situation. I got talked into it one more time years later when Lew Perkins, whom I had inherited as a player at Iowa, became athletic director at Wichita State. "Come on, Ralph," he said. "Everybody back there wants you to come back and play."

I got soft-hearted and made the deal. On this occasion, I was the loser. My worst Oregon State team, the one in 1985-1986, traveled back to Wichita and blew a late lead and lost. We had Wichita two years later at our place but dropped that one, too.

I established a first at Iowa by getting kicked out of the first game of my life there—and on one technical foul. Dick Schultz was my assistant. Well, Dick was as quiet, mild-mannered, and efficient then as a coach as he seems today as the executive director of the NCAA. We were at Michigan State, and we had three officials then that you'd have to classify as homers.

We were getting beat, but I tried to keep myself under control. I had developed something of a reputation as a bench jockey. Frank Henkel at Wichita East used to laugh and say that he had to yank me back down to my seat by the coattails.

Everything was quiet until one of my players dribbled down to the foul line, made a bucket, then was fouled. Well, this official came rushing up, cancelled the basket, then gave us two free-throws. Dick got up as the official came to report the play to the scorer's table, and asked, "Why doesn't the basket count?"

The official says, "Sit down, or I'll give you a technical."

"I will sit down," Dick said, "but you have to tell me why the basket didn't count."

Boom, technical foul on Dick. That ended my patience. In one leap, I was over to the official, nose to nose. I never opened my mouth, and he slammed a technical on me and kicked me out. My first technical foul that night and I get kicked out of the game. I happened to run into Herm Rorig, the Big Ten supervisor of officials, a couple of weeks later. He said he was still waiting for my report of the incident. I told him he was going to wait until I saw the official's report.

"He said you called him a bad name," Herm said.

"If he had given me a few more seconds," I said, "I might have."

But the greatest story I ever heard about a basketball coach getting kicked out occurred in Texas in a junior college game. The coach got three technicals, and was kicked out. There was a window high up in the gym, and he decided he could see the game if he got a ladder. One of the officials saw him looking up through the window and slapped a fourth technical foul on him.

I don't think I deserved my technical, and I don't think that fellow deserved to get his fourth, either.

The 1966-1967 season would have brought us a piece of the Big Ten title—and an automatic berth in the NCAA because we had been away longest—but for a triple-overtime loss at home.

We had gone 20-3 at home my first two years at Iowa, and had a home-court win streak of 21 games before Wisconsin came to town in February. A 96-95 loss in three overtimes knocked us out of a share of the Big Ten lead with Indiana and Michigan State.

We hung in the rest of the race, and entering the final day, had a slender chance to create a three-way tie for the title. We beat Michigan with Sam Williams scoring 28, but Indiana handled Purdue and Michigan State beat Northwestern, leaving us a game behind.

Williams scored 22.7 points a game to lead us in scoring, Gerry Jones— eligible for his senior season—was our MVP, and we compiled a 16-8 record. We were third place with a 9-5 record, the third straight year of first-division finishes. If we were tired of third place, we would take care of that the next season.

9

Stalking Championships

The 1967-1968 Iowa team has always been one of my favorites. Aside from Sam Williams, who had scored 25 points a game in Big Ten play the season before, we were starting over again. Sam was a player, but you couldn't consider the rest of them good basketball players, at least at that stage of their development. Sam was the key, and the rest of them played their roles.

This is how we put that team together: Dick Jensen was from the little Iowa town of Madrid. He was the nicest kid in the world, and the best scorer in the history of the state as a high school senior. He didn't turn out to be much of a scorer in college, but he was a good solid player. He played good defense and concentrated on the backboards.

Then, with the help of Lanny Van Eman, and our old connection in McKeesport with Neenie Campbell, we tapped into that area. Out came Glenn Vidnovic from McKeesport and Chad Calabria from Aliquippa. Vidnovic we called the Stick. He was one of the thinnest players imaginable, about 6'6" and maybe 165 pounds. He was rangy and a very good defensive player. He joined us at the mid-semester break that season. Calabria was sort of the off-guard type, about 6'2", and like many western Pennsylvania kids, seemingly very tough and hard-nosed. We also had Huston Breedlove, a 6'6" forward, and two hustling guards, Ron Norman and Rolly McGrath. There was no great talent there, other than Williams.

Some Birthday Present

That was surely one of the wildest Big Ten seasons ever. Purdue, with the great shooter Rick Mount, went into the season as a co-favorite with Indiana. We were picked for third by the writers, and fourth by the coaches. Ohio State was selected for no better than sixth. By the end of the season, Indiana found itself in a tie for last. We lost to three teams that ended in a tie for sixth. Ohio State, which finished as a co-champion with us, lost to Minnesota and beat Indiana by a point—the teams that finished tied for the basement.

Certainly there was nothing very remarkable about the way we started. I always called December our month for education, no matter where I was, and this was one of those. We got off with two wins against Bowling Green and Jack Hartman's Southern Illinois team, but then on a swing to the West before the Los Angeles Classic, we lost a couple of close games to California and Stanford. After we got back from the tournament, we lost our league opener on the road to Northwestern.

We were 5-5 and apparently bound for a pretty mediocre season. We got back on track with three straight wins at home against Loyola of Chicago, Ohio State in overtime, and Minnesota. Then we beat Michigan State, 76-71, ending the Spartans' 25-game winning streak at home, and found ourselves sharing first place in the Big Ten. At that point, we dropped one to Illinois, but then we hit our stride. In our next eight games, we won seven, avenging the loss to Illinois and losing only to Purdue on the road.

Now we had a stranglehold, if a perilous one, on the Big Ten lead. An Ohio State team led by Bill Hosket and Steve Howell was chasing us, half a game behind. We had brought it down to this: On my 49th birthday, March 9, all we had to do was beat a second-division Michigan team at home to claim the Big Ten title outright. Ohio State was finished, waiting to see what happened to us.

What happened to us was one of the most disappointing games in my career. Michigan, a 15-point underdog, burst to a 15-2 lead. We missed our first 11 shots. It seems that we had made comments after our 13-point win at Michigan that we believed we had won because we were in better physical shape, and now

Michigan was exacting its revenge. The lead reached 27-11.

We did edge back to within 40-32 at halftime, but it was just one of those days. Even when Rudy Tomjanovich, Michigan's big star, sprained his ankle with 14 minutes to go, we could not make up the difference.

We did try. Sam Williams had 30 points and 14 rebounds, and with our sell-out crowd of 12,900 screaming, we made a run. Williams got us within a point with two free throws, but Michigan then edged to a 71-68 lead with 1:40 left. Vidnovic was called for a charge, and Michigan evened it out by making a turnover. Again, we got within one point on Norman's jump shot inside the last minute.

We had a final chance. Michigan missed a free throw and we worked for the shot that would send us into the NCAA tournament, but we threw the ball away and that was it—a 71-70 loss. Some birthday present.

We found ourselves co-champions with Ohio State, staring at a playoff at West Lafayette for the NCAA berth at Lexington, Kentucky. The irony of the situation was that had this happened a year earlier, we would have taken the trip to the NCAAs. Until 1968 the Big Ten rule stipulated that the tied team that had made the tournament most recently was eliminated, and that was Ohio State. However, the rule was changed, and it mandated a playoff, the first one in the conference in 60 years.

I didn't feel optimistic, and my fears were realized. We had another one of those terrible starts, missing our first ten shots and going the first eight minutes without a field goal. We were down by six at halftime, and Ohio State kept control and developed a 12-point lead with two minutes left.

Then we made a great comeback, cutting the deficit to two before a couple of free throws for Ohio State made it an 85-81 final. Sam Williams, playing his final game for us, had a 29-point, 18-rebound night. The topper was, we couldn't get off the Purdue campus that night. There was a major snowstorm that grounded both teams.

Talk about mixed feelings. We had had a wonderful season, surprising most people, winning a co-championship in the Big Ten and going 16-9 overall. Sam Williams won conference most valuable player honors, averaging 25.6 points a game and leading us in scoring 20 of 25 games. But that Michigan loss was galling. We wouldn't have gone very far in the regionals, but we would have at least earned the right.

That plum would have to come later.

Cold Players in a Cold Season

The less said about the 1968-1969 season, the better. Unfortunately, I said quite a bit about it before it ever got there. I really thought that team was ready for some big things. True, we lost Sam Williams, but we had several key players back — Vidnovic, Calabria, Norman, Jensen, and Chris Philips. Ben McGilmer had returned from the service — albeit with a knee injury that limited his huge potential — and we had added an excellent recruit, John Johnson, a Milwaukee product by way of Northwest Wyoming Junior College. I said that I thought our prospects were very good.

We didn't have that quarterback type of guard, but to this day, I believe there might have been another reason for our problems, a weird one. The team used to practice in an old building warmed up with portable heaters. I walked into the place about four or five days before practice and there were no heaters there.

"What's going on?" I asked the man in charge. "We've got no heaters in this place."

"Well, gee," he said. "the guy who was supposed to be handling it retired July 1. He never told anybody else, so we have no heaters."

We decided to just live with it. It gets cold in Iowa, bitterly cold. At times, we used thick jackets and football warmups with the old hoods on, and we stationed a sunlamp in each corner of the floor. I don't think we ever did get the team in shape. I didn't want to have them getting colds and flu, so many nights we cut practice short. We goofed.

We just didn't jell like we should have. We never won a conference road game and ended up losing eight of our last ten. The final tally was a 12-12 overall record and 5-9 in the Big Ten, each of them my worst in six years there. J.J., John Johnson, made a big impact, leading us in scoring at 19.7 a game with an average of ten rebounds.

It wasn't a good season, but there was plenty to look forward to.

If the foundation for the 1969-1970 Iowa team wasn't laid during the tough times of 1968-1969, then it happened when we ventured over to a JC tournament in Iowa to watch a prospect there. We knew Freddie Brown was a player. He was from Milwaukee, like J.J., but they had gone to different high schools and Fred was a year younger. We knew of Fred in high school, but he couldn't qualify. This was back in the days where they used a 1.7 grade-point scale to predict whether a person would qualify for college. So Fred went to Burlington Junior College. We put him there, and Fred didn't even know it. We told the coach at Burlington, "He's one of the best guards you'll ever have. You go up to Milwaukee and get Freddie."

And he did.

But Dick Schultz and Lanny Van Eman couldn't make up their minds whether we ought to take him or not. They thought he might be too much to handle. We had a senior-dominated team coming back, and sometimes a JC player, wanting to play right away, can be disruptive to such a group.

Finally, they said, "Coach, you've got to go see him."

Well, we drove to a regional tournament about 100 miles away. At halftime, I said, "Let's go."

We get back to Iowa City and Lanny asked me, "What are you going to do with him?"

"You take him," I said. "I'll handle him. He's a player."

And he was. A marvelous shooter, he became known, of course, as Downtown Freddie Brown. He might have been as good a passer as he was a shooter. He also had the longest hang time of anybody I've ever seen. He could go up in the air, get in trouble, and get out before he came back down.

However, I sold him on something else. I told him, "You know, until you got to be 20 points ahead in that game, you were the finest defensive guard I've seen in a long, long time. So this is what I'm going to do for you. I'm going to make you the finest defensive guard in the Big Ten."

He did indeed become a very intuitive defensive player, but that 1970 Iowa team would do some things on offense that would make fans take their minds off defense.

J.J. and the Dealers

It is hard to attach too many superlatives to that 1970 team. It was simply the best passing team I've ever had, the best passing team I ever saw. There's the old passing rule that it's the responsibility of the receiver to get open, and everybody on that team knew how to get open. The action could just flow. The 1970 team was the only team I ever saw that could walk and fast-break at the same time. Somebody was always shooting within three feet of the basket before it was over. The press took to calling the club "J.J. and the Dealers."

We haven't had too many people that could pass the way J.J. could, and he was 6'7", a force on the backboards, as well. In fact, J.J. was one of those guys that made it tough on me because I was always railing on the bounce pass, something I did until my retirement. J.J. liked the bounce pass, and he was one of the few who could do it well with consistency. So I had to say, "Look, John, I know you can do the bounce pass, but if I start letting you do it, I'm going to have problems. So let's put this rule into effect: If you absolutely have to use it, use it. But there better be no other way for you to pass."

J.J. followed instructions.

John was one of the flattest shooters in America. He played his whole career that way. I'd been trying to get him to put more arch in his shot, but he'd just say, "Aw, come on, coach, I've shot it this way all my life."

It didn't take long for John to make an impact. In his third game at Iowa in the 1968-1969 season against Wisconsin-Milwaukee, he scored 46 points to topple the Hawkeye scoring record established almost 25 years prior by Dick Ives in 1944. J.J. even managed to learn a lesson about flat shooting. John had tied Ives' record with about nine minutes left, then he proceeded to miss four straight free throws and four field-goal attempts before finally getting a three-point play to break the record. We pulled him out with five and a half minutes left.

Next practice, he came in and said, "Coach, you're right, I need a little help with my shot. Let's get to work."

John was a leader. We played in the Rainbow Classic in Honolulu late in December, and had a hard time getting home. We flew back on New Year's Eve, and when we got back there was two feet of snow on the ground and it was below zero outside. There was a strike among airline baggage-handlers so when we finally arrived back in Iowa City, it was five in the morning. We had to play Purdue, the defending Big Ten champion, within 48 hours so we had to practice sometime that day.

It was New Year's Day. I figured we'd just throw it open to the kids and let them decide when they wanted to practice. I said, "We've got a choice. We can get off the bus, walk into the fieldhouse, and practice right now. Or we can go home, go to bed, come back in the afternoon. If we do that, we miss some of the bowl games. What's your decision?"

"No question about that, right, guys?" J.J. says. "We practice now, right?"

At six in the morning, after traveling all night on the plane, we went out and practiced about 75 minutes. That's all we could stand.

For quite awhile, there didn't appear to be anything very special about that team. We opened the year by losing at Southern Illinois. We won at home against St. Francis of Pennsylvania and Duquesne, but then we lost to Cincinnati, and Creighton at home. The first inkling that we might be coming together was a 101-78 victory over Drake, who would go on to win the Missouri Valley championship that year.

On to Hawaii. St. John's beat us by two when somebody threw in a 25-foot hook shot with a couple of seconds left. We got out of the Islands with a lopsided victory over Hawaii, but through December, we were only 4-4.

Yet there were some signs. Dick Jensen had been slowed by mononucleosis. Freddie had been bothered by an allergy. But by January, we appeared ready. We had had the benefit of a month with Fred meshing into the system and certainly we had a lot of experience. As Fred said, we were off and running once he got familiar with the scheme.

John Johnson: "When we lost the heartbreaker to St. John's, I knew then we were going to win the Big Ten. That's how confident I was about our team. We kept getting better and

better and better. After we got Freddie used to the system, we could just destroy teams with the man-to-man press and the trapping press. Freddie probably played the passing lanes better than anybody I've ever seen except Jerry West. And Freddie averaged almost 21 points a game in the Big Ten and was thought of as a playmaker.

"There were no big egos, it didn't matter who scored. Vidnovic, the Stick, was totally intimidating with those long arms. Dick Jensen was a pretty fair rebounder and a great position defensive player. Ben McGilmer was a great shooter, he could pop out to 20 feet. Chad was something of everything, probably best suited to off-guard. He was somebody who would walk through hell with gasoline underwear on. He couldn't wait for the game to start, he was so pumped up.

"Maybe the unique thing was, with Glenn and me at forward, we handled the ball more than our guards. It gave us an added dimension. And our big guys could shoot.

"The 1969 team didn't have a lot of speed so Ralph was kind of apprehensive about letting us run with the basketball. But as the season progressed, and we got Freddie the following year, we kind of pinched him, coerced him into letting us run. After he did that, the results were rave reviews. The only thing Ralph had to do was sit back and make substitutions."

The Conference Leaders

We managed to slide past Purdue, 94-88, in that Big Ten opener. Rick Mount, as usual, was our biggest problem. He scored 53 points, giving him an average of 42 points against us in five games. He was absolutely one of the greatest pure shooters that ever stepped on a court. He had 40-foot range, and 35 was a snap. Everything else was like a lay-up. He was the only one-handed shooter I've ever seen with that range.

But that game was typical of my career-long philosophy: One man isn't going to beat you. He had to take 43 shots to get that 53, and as long as we made him work, and didn't let the others get out of hand, we were all right. We also caught a break in that Larry Weatherford, their No. 2 scorer that season, and Bill Franklin, the Purdue starting center, were held out of the game in a disciplinary action.

Soon we were rolling. We went to Ann Arbor, and illustrated what a good club we were offensively. We created only nine turnovers that day, yet shot a school-record 63.4 percent and won 107-99 to exact a bit of revenge for three straight losses to Michigan, including that disappointing season-ending game in 1968. Rudy Tomjanovich got 37 points for Michigan, but we had 34 from J.J., 24 from Calabria, 23 from Brown and 18 from Vidnovic. We had some weapons.

On we marched. It became a story when we didn't score 100 points. We got out to a 51-22 lead at halftime at Madison—in what I called the best half of basketball any of my teams had ever played on the road—and won 92-74. We added a non-league win at home against Tennessee Tech and then hit the century mark again against Indiana at home, 100-93, when Vidnovic scored 31. We were in the midst of a stretch when we shot better than 50 percent in nine straight games.

At 4-0 in the conference, we were still a breath behind Illinois, who was 5-0 and 12-3. But on the night when we beat Bill Fitch's Minnesota team 90-77 at home, with J.J. scoring 33, Wisconsin surprised Illinois on the road, ending a two-year home-court winning streak for the Illini, and we took over the conference lead. We wouldn't be giving it up.

10

Marked Men in the Big Ten

We went on the road to Bloomington, shot 61 percent and thrashed Indiana, 104-89, with J.J. getting another 33. We were now marked men in the Big Ten, and we got pelted with debris there, including coins. At home, we whipped Wisconsin, 119-100, setting a school scoring record in getting off to a 7-0 conference start, best at Iowa in 26 years. We had four players scoring 20 or more points in that game, and one of them, Ben McGilmer, didn't even start.

We were halfway through the Big Ten season, and I knew we had something very good going. Yet our defense wasn't playing that well, and we had some very difficult road games ahead, including Illinois, Ohio State, and Purdue, so I wasn't getting too giddy.

Ralph the Ripper

About this time, we began having a terrible time with a few people in the Big Ten believing we were too merciless in our play. With all our offensive and defensive tools, we would hear charges that we were running up the score needlessly on our opponents. Don't think that this was something new. My teams weren't always good enough to warrant this accusation, but charges of running it up date back quite awhile. Way back in 1952, shortly after my second game as a college coach, Bill Hodge wrote in the *Wichita Eagle:*

"They'll be calling him Ralph the Ripper one of these days, if they don't start now, because he doesn't shave points for the benefit of an opponent . . .

"For the second time within nine months, a Miller-coached team ran the score into three digits Wednesday night to satisfy a hungry desire to set scoring records. Round No. two was the University of Wichita's 100-63 walloping of the Creighton University Blue Jays.

"In round one last March at the same Forum court, Miller's Wichita East High Aces walloped the Arkansas City Bulldogs, 105-35 . . . the new Shocker mentor was criticized by some Ark Valley coaches last winter for refusing to call off his stars when he had his opponent hopelessly beaten . . . "

I've heard this throughout my career. George Raveling was upset one time early in his tenure at Washington State when we continued to use our full-court defenses late in the game. Ned Wulk at Arizona State felt similarly after we beat his team soundly in 1982. I consider both of them good friends today. George was one of my favorites. Ned had surgery last spring, and Jean and I went to see him during the Pac-10 tournament.

Many people have felt that we ran it up. It goes back to the first full year I coached. We were playing at Dodge City, Kansas, in a tournament against a little school called Pretty Prairie. The coach was a former teammate of mine at KU. In those days, there were only ten players. Well, we could have beaten them with my second five, and we had to play a 32-minute game. In the first five minutes, I think it was 22-1. I ran people in and out, and my second group played just as well as my first. I did everything but tell people not to shoot. I did everything to keep the score within reason, except going into ball control with a 40-point lead or telling my kids not to shoot, and I don't think that would have been very smart. Boy, did my friend give me heck for running up the score.

I'll admit that my judgment on what constitutes running up the score differs from that of many people. Start with this premise: A coach is nothing but a teacher. I could never quite see the idea of having one team play one way and having a group of subs play another way. So when our subs went in, they would be pressing in the last 30 seconds, just as our regulars did. Maybe this is wrong.

The other point is, I was always more worried about what my team did, not theirs. I guess that's gotten me in trouble on occasion. If another coach ran the score up on me, I can't say that it bothered me. My real worry was about how my team played, not how the other coach decided to play the last few minutes of the game.

I remember my first year at Oregon State. We took a decimated team to Los Angeles near the end of the season. We played UCLA first and got beat 94-64. I don't remember John Wooden slowing down the fast-break. Then we went over to play Bob Boyd's USC outfit. USC had the second best team in the nation. I thought they played a beautiful ball game. They beat us 110-75, and many people said, "Bob really ran up the score on you, didn't he?"

I said, "Well, no more than John did. I didn't think he ran up the score. You know, we're pretty bad."

I didn't think anything about it. Put yourself in Bob's shoes. He had the No. 2 team in the country. He was fighting against the No. 1 team right across town. I'm sorry, but if I'd been Bob, my team would have played the same way.

At Wichita one time, a coach accused me of running up the score, and shortly after, we found ourselves playing a Big Ten team that had just played Kansas and Kansas State. Well, I remembered what I'd been told, and I called off the dogs and only beat them by 17 points. We could have beaten them by 35 or 40. We were rewarded by this observation in the paper: "Yeah, Wichita has a good ball club, but they're not as good as Kansas or Kansas State."

To each his own.

> **Ned Wulk: "In my last year, they beat us something awful, and I did not understand. I think he was somewhat shorthanded, and I didn't think he had done much substituting under the circumstances. I wasn't a very good loser, I guess. I regretted the outburst. It was a frustrating**

night on which we got totally humiliated, and I
guess I got humiliated, too. I don't think Ralph
and I had any difficulty after that. I think we had
played against each other so many years, we
couldn't hold those things over for so long."

Championship Bound

They had installed new scoreboards, featuring room for three
digits in the Iowa Fieldhouse just before that season, and it was
a good thing. We tested them. We won our tenth game in a row
against Michigan State, 103-77, with J.J. getting 36 points and
Freddie 25 in a game in which we scored 63 in the second half. We
broke the game open near the finish, and Gus Ganakas, the MSU
coach, got upset because he thought we poured it on.

One of our biggest games of the season was next. We had
risen to 11th in the Associated Press poll, but would face Illinois
at Champaign, where we hadn't won since 1962. It was a hard-
fought game in which we led by one at halftime and simply
toughed it out. Freddie had 22 points and J.J. had 19 rebounds.
Those efforts, combined with our foul shooting, were the big
difference. We hit 17 of 19 from the line, which wasn't unchar-
acteristic for that team. We shot 78 percent, which still stands as
the season record at Iowa.

Ohio State, on the road, was our next test. That was a Buckeye
team that shared some traits with our club. It was 6-3 in the Big
Ten and leading the nation entering the game in both field-goal
percentage and free throw shooting, at 55 and 81.

We survived. J.J. had 38 points, his high for the season at that
point, and we really outmuscled them with a 50-33 edge in
rebounds. Again, we were hardly the darlings of the conference
when we went on the road. Somebody threw a large orange from
somewhere in St. John Arena and it missed McGilmer's head by
a few inches.

Now we were 10-0 and beginning to smell the Big Ten
championship. Purdue was still a threat at 8-2. We had to go to
West Lafayette shortly, but we knew we had the makings to win
the championship outright and avoid the disappointment of
1968.

In our next game, John Johnson was unstoppable. Against Northwestern, we began by forcing 12 turnovers in the first 12 minutes. We scored nine points in a span of 41 seconds in the first half, keyed by our defense. But it was J.J. who scored an Iowa-record 49 points—another mark that still stands—on 20 of 33 field goals and nine of ten from the foul line. We had three games to go and were 11-0, but Purdue was still 9-2, and we would go there next.

I think people today would tell you our game with Purdue was one of the all-timers in the Big Ten. Obviously, still in the hunt for the title, they were ready to play, and so were we. There was a full house at Mackey Arena. The Boilermakers had won 19 straight league games at home and 30 overall on their floor.

Rick Mount scored Purdue's first five baskets, and that would be a trend. Weatherford, the second leading scorer, got his third foul just five minutes into the game, and fans began throwing paper onto the floor. They were warned that the next time they did it, it would warrant a technical foul.

We were behind by ten with a little more than four minutes left in the half, but our fast-break began clicking and we took a 49-47 lead to the locker room. Mount had 32 points—at half. It was still close when, with 13 minutes left in the game, a Purdue player was called for a foul and a wadded-up program came tumbling onto the floor. Technical foul on Purdue. You don't see it very often; there have been many instances where the crowd is warned but rarely do you see a team actually penalized for the crowd action.

There was some dark speculation that the program had come from the Iowa section, but we'll never know. I do know there were only 24 seats allotted Iowa so the odds were certainly against the program having been thrown by a Hawk fan. At any rate, the technical foul was part of a six-point play during which Purdue never touched the ball. Calabria hit the free throw and Vidnovic hit a jumper and we led 73-70.

That didn't hold up. Purdue came back and led us, 101-92, inside the five-minute mark. Brown led us back into a one-point lead at 104-103 with 62 seconds left. Then Purdue went back ahead, 105-104, on a field goal with just 37 seconds left.

J.J. came right back for us with one of those clothesline jumpers, and now came the telling blow. Purdue shot, missed, and Vidnovic rebounded and was fouled with 10 seconds left. He downed both free throws, and we led 108-105. He said later he had one thought on his mind: Championship. Indeed, it was ours, after we allowed Purdue to hit a final basket for the 108-107 score. There was a piece of poetic justice in it for us, because Purdue had clinched the Big Ten title at our place in 1969 on the way to a national-runner-up finish.

Mount had had a phenomenal day, scoring 61 points, a Big Ten record. He took 47 shots and hit 27 of them. This was a time when there were some amazing individual performances. A couple of weeks before this, Pete Maravich hit 64 for Louisiana State, and Dan Issel had 51 for Kentucky in the same game.

John Johnson, laughing: "Rick Mount was the greatest pure shooter I've ever seen. Freddie is a hell of a shooter, but he couldn't shoot with Rick Mount. His range was unbelievable. It's frightening to think what he would have done with the three-point shot in effect.

"We used to tease Fred, that Fred was watching him out there."

Fred Brown: "Our scouting report had J.J., Vidnovic or Calabria to guard Mount. None of those guys wanted to guard him so I volunteered. Every time J.J. brings it up, I tell him, remember who got you here, we won the game."

So the championship was ours, although we very much wanted to close out the regular season undefeated. In a pretty typical performance, we beat Ohio State, 113-92, at our place, shooting 58 percent and 90 percent from the line. J.J. had 37, Brown 24. Vidnovic had 14 rebounds to lead everyone.

I admitted after the game that I wasn't totally satisfied, inasmuch as we allowed Ohio State to shoot 53 percent. "I guess I'm getting a little greedy," I told the press. "I want them to do everything perfectly. But if you're going to get greedy, you might as well get greedy as hell."

Only two teams since the mid-1930s—Ohio State's great 1961 club with Jerry Lucas and John Havlicek, and the 1943 Illinois Whiz Kids, coached by Doug Mills—had made it through a Big Ten season unbeaten. We would be the third, although Northwestern didn't go down easily at Evanston. We trailed by ten late in the half and were on top only by a point, 81-80. But we stretched it out with what would become a 63-point second half and won 115-101. J.J. had 32 points—although Northwestern played a box-and-one defense on him part of the time—to become Iowa's highest single-season scorer.

The National Title and Fate

We had 16 victories in a row at that point, one away from the 17 the 1955-1956 Fabulous Five team at Iowa had run up in going all the way to the championship game against San Francisco. We certainly had come a long way since early December. Nobody knew that better than Al Grady, the sports editor for the *Iowa City Press-Citizen*. At that time when we were struggling, he wrote, "Maybe Iowa isn't any better than that. Maybe this team is playing about as well as it can be expected to play. I hope I am wrong. I would like nothing better than to eat a copy of this column in March while preparing to go to the NCAA tournament with the Hawkeyes."

Well, we obliged Al. During the week before the tournament, we invited him over to the gym. Calabria applied a bottle of ketchup to the column, and Al chowed down in front of a photographer from his paper.

Our next assignment was Jacksonville, one of the biggest college teams ever, in the Mideast Regional at Columbus. I suppose in today's scheme of seeding the NCAA teams, this matchup would never come about. We were ranked seventh, and obviously hot. Jacksonville was fourth. Kentucky, who would play Notre Dame in the other game in the regional, was top-ranked. It was simply a loaded regional.

Jacksonville had Artis Gilmore, the longtime pro, at 7'2", and Pembrook Burrows at 7'0". Yet I was confident. We were so effective with our press, and our passing and shooting, that we were capable of offsetting such a huge height disadvantage. Well, we did have trouble with all that size. By halftime, Gilmore had 20 points, three blocked shots, and had goal-tended three others. But this one wouldn't be decided early. It was 50-49, Jacksonville, at the half.

We got Artis out of the game on fouls with eight minutes left, but Jacksonville hung tough and expanded a short lead to eight— the biggest spread of a high-scoring game—with five minutes left. Then, just as he had done in the Purdue game, Freddie led us back as Jacksonville tried to stall. He downed three straight long jumpers, and when Calabria hit a couple of free throws, it was 100-all with a minute left.

Now Brown was fouled, but he made just one of two, and when Rex Morgan scored from the key with 41 seconds remaining, Jacksonville was back on top 102-101. On a night when he scored 27 to lead us, Freddie took a long shot, rebounded it and nudged it back in for our final basket of the night, and we led 103-102, just 18 seconds from the finish.

Then, as I've always put it, the fickle hand of fate took over. Vaughn Wedeking, who went just two for eight for the night, came down and hurried up a 30-foot shot from out on top with six seconds left. No way. Ohio State's rims are the toughest in America. A shot that long can go just about anywhere.

We've got everybody blocked off, even Pembrook, but he jumped up, scrapes the ball—I'm not sure he got more than a fingernail on it—it goes back up on the rim, teeters back and topples in just before the buzzer. We lose.

The ride was over, and I felt bad. Our team could have won the national title. St. Bonaventure went on to the Final Four, but it had lost Bob Lanier to a knee injury. Jacksonville gave UCLA a good game for the championship, but I think we could have beaten them. It was just another tough pill to swallow.

John Johnson: "First of all, we're going to Columbus and the damn engine in the plane went off. We got there, and there was a snow-storm. We arrived at the hotel—Fred and I were roommates—and it was hot and stuffy. We watched TV, opened the windows, and left them

open all night. I catch a damn cold, get sicker than a dog.

"Lanny gave us the scouting report on Jacksonville, and it said Pembrook Burrows couldn't shoot. They played him at the high post and Artis low. So we're sagging to help out on Artis, and Pembrook Burrows shot 11 out of 12 that night.

"I wholeheartedly agree, we would have won the national championship without a doubt. I told Sidney Wicks to his face what would have happened that year. We would have matched up perfectly with UCLA, because Vidnovic and I were much more versatile players than Sidney Wicks and Curtis Rowe. They were bigger than we were, but as far as being matched up and playing a full-court game, no way. With Steve Patterson, they didn't have a big center. And our guards would have killed John Vallely and Henry Bibby."

Consolation

We left one more calling card, something for the college-basketball world to remember us by, in what turned out to be a grand catharsis of our frustrations over Jacksonville. These were the days of the consolation game, now gone by the boards. It didn't mean anything, just a final game to salve one team's wounds.

Johnny Dee was the Notre Dame coach. The Irish had lost 109-99 to Adolph Rupp's Kentucky team the night Jacksonville beat us. Asked about playing Iowa, Johnny said, "Well, Iowa's got a good ball club, but we've already played three or four Big Ten teams and we've beaten them all."

I didn't like that comment. I told our team, "I want you to do me a favor and take care of Johnny Dee a little bit."

Well, I couldn't ask for anything better. I almost felt sorry for Johnny by halftime—but not too much. More than that, I guess the team was genuinely moved by what I had told them on the day between games.

"That was the first time in four years I've heard that man talk like that," said Calabria. "It was a very emotional speech, about how sorry he was for us that we hadn't been able to go on. No one said a thing out loud. We knew we wanted to give this one to our coach."

Did they ever. We had a 53-22 lead with seven minutes to play in the first half. Talk about an offense machine. It was one of the greatest displays of fluidity and teamwork ever. Adolph Rupp, whose Kentucky team was playing in the second game, got to the arena, looked up, saw the score and thought he was late, that it must have been the second half.

Johnny Dee called three timeouts in the first eight and a half minutes, and we led 75-42 at halftime. There wasn't much I needed to say then, only a halfhearted admonition of J.J., who had passed behind his back and between his legs. "J.J.," I said, "I think everybody knows you can pass behind your back now."

At the finish, we had eased off the throttle and won, 121-106, establishing a scoring record in NCAA play that would stand until Oklahoma beat it in 1989. Calabria hit 15 of 22 shots for 31 points. J.J. had 31 and Vidnovic 24.

We rewrote the Iowa record book that year. There were 18 school records, 12 by the team, and five individual ones by J.J. Maybe Bill Hodge, a little-used reserve guard, summed it up most poignantly: "There were times," he said, "when I didn't think I was good enough to belong on that team."

Me, I was off to a new challenge. But I wouldn't soon forget that club.

Part IV
Coaching at
Oregon State

11

Transition and Tragedy

I suppose one of the reasons we left Iowa was that the 1970 team played at the Rainbow Classic that season. My family and I loved Iowa, and I loved working for the university. It was a great six years, but Iowa weather can be brutal. Winters are severe; summers are hot and humid. Many people learn to live with it, but when I saw the other side of the world, it gave me pause. We flew out of Des Moines to Honolulu under blizzard conditions. We spent an extra two hours in Des Moines because it was that long before they could get a charter plane to pick us up.

We were in Honolulu for a week, and it was great—beautiful sunshine. Jean and the children basked on the beach. After it was over, we had the long flight back and when we arrived home, there was an even worse blizzard than when we left. For three or four weeks in a row, the mean temperature was well below zero.

About the middle of that period, I came home and Jean told me that there had to be someplace in the United States where it was warm and they needed a basketball coach. I couldn't disagree.

Associations with Oregon State

I actually had a limited association with Oregon State since the Wichita State days. It stemmed from a game in 1958 played in Corvallis when Oregon State beat us handily. Jim Anderson, my assistant for 19 years at OSU, played in that game. During the course of the game, Ron Heller, our forward, got decked and came down on the back of his head. He didn't get up. Les Needham, our trainer, was sitting next to me, but Les didn't move.

So I said, "Hey, Doc, go out and see what's wrong."

Well, Ron was OK, but Doc Needham, in walking back to the bench—he had to cover about two-thirds of the court—was reeling like a drunken man, walking in S shapes.

"Doc, don't you feel well?" I asked him.

"Oh yeah," he said. "Fine."

Halftime came shortly after that. There are concrete steps down to the locker room at Gill Coliseum. I had a player, Ev Wessel, 6'9", who had torn up his knee in a game in Eugene just before. Strongest young man I ever met in my life.

Just as we started down the steps, Doc collapsed and pitched forward. Ev reached out and caught Doc by the collar with one hand and kept him from falling. We took Doc down into the locker room, and it was one of the worst halftimes I ever spent. We didn't have a team doctor with us. We had to get one. We did, but it took most of halftime. The kids were just sitting there, and Doc was totally out of it.

It turned out he had had a stroke. During the course of the evening and the next morning, he had nine more and died not long after. Spec Keene was the athletic director at Oregon State at that time, and was wonderful to us. He made arrangements to get Doc's wife there, and I stayed an extra two days. I had a warm feeling in my heart for the people at Oregon State.

Rumors and Coincidence

Another factor in my departure—though I wouldn't call it a large one—was a nasty feud going on in the Iowa athletic department. Ironically, as we were making our great run through the Big Ten that winter of 1970, there were almost daily newspaper stories on the deteriorating relationship between Forest Evashevski, the athletic director, and Ray Nagel, the football coach. It was referred to as a power struggle.

During the problems, several coaches resigned and there was an investigation of the football operations. Finally, the feud ended bitterly. The school's athletic board fired Ray and accepted Evy's resignation. Both of them came out losers in the deal. Evy was considered a controversial person by many people, but he was still one of my best friends. I never worked for a stronger person, or a man I liked more than I liked Evy. There wasn't a ripple of trouble between us. Today we consider ourselves good friends with both the Evashevskis and Nagels.

Perhaps the split in loyalties was one more reason to leave. It gets very tiring being in the middle. It was a tumultuous year for Iowa athletics. In the span of a few months, the school had to replace an athletic director, a football coach, and a basketball coach.

These were still the days when there was a semblance of stability in coaching. You didn't have quite the willy-nilly scramble of jobs that you do today. The year I came to Oregon State, there weren't very many jobs open. But I did hear of one when my father-in-law, Morris, wrote a letter to me at Iowa from Redlands, California, asking if we knew that somebody in Oregon had resigned. We didn't even know who it was.

We went on to the NCAA at Maryland. Staying in Washington, D.C., I ran into Tex Winter, a longtime coaching associate, and asked him who had resigned in the state of Oregon. He said it was Paul Valenti, who had coached Oregon State the past six years.

"Do they have any representatives here?" I asked.

"Yes, Paul's here, and the athletic director, Jim Barratt."

"Well, if you see them, just tell them if they're interested in a basketball coach, let me know."

Shortly after this exchange, Barratt initiated contact. During the course of that conversation, we came to a general agreement. Of course, I would have to come back to the athletic board at Oregon State for approval, but he didn't think that would be a problem. The stage was set, and nothing was said to anybody except Evy.

The final list of candidates included Dick Edwards, the head coach at University of Pacific; Ted Wilson of Linfield College; Les Habegger of Seattle Pacific; Jim Anderson, Paul Valenti's assistant coach; and me.

Little did we know what we were in for. A story appeared in the *Corvallis Gazette-Times*, saying that I would be named the next coach. The athletic board wasn't happy with that, and subsequently wrestled with the choice, deadlocking over Edwards and me. Round and round it went, with no resolution. We had been there a few days and were getting impatient after what we thought would be little more than a rubber-stamp approval.

We spent a Sunday while they were mulling things over and they still weren't able to come to a conclusion, so I told Mr. Barratt, "In this case, take my name off the roster. I've got a job, I don't need this one."

The headline in the next morning's *Oregonian* newspaper read: "Valenti's Successor Not Miller." We departed Corvallis Sunday night, fully intending never to have anything to do with the Oregon State job. Only a fluke caused me to return.

We spent Sunday night in Portland and flew out Monday morning for Kansas City. The plan had been for Jean to pick up our car—which we had left in Kansas City—drive down to Chanute, pick up the kids, and then return the next day to Iowa City. In the meantime, I would just fly home from Kansas City to Iowa City and be in by late afternoon.

But Jean said, "You know, I'm just too tired to do this by myself."

So I said, "That's OK, I'll go with you. I'll call Evy and tell him we'll be a day late."

We arrived in Chanute, spent Monday night there, and drove all day Tuesday back to Iowa City. In the middle of the night, the phone rang. Jim Barratt. It was at least 2:00 a.m. Central time. I think Jim forgot about the time difference. Well, I told him I'd call him back in the morning. Jean and I and our two children there, Paul and Shannon, decided it was a good proposition, better weather, and we would take it.

First thing in the morning, I called Evy to tell him I took the Oregon State job after all, and in his office was a very good and influential friend of Evy and me.

"I want to talk to Ralph," he says. "He's going to stay here."

"It's not going to do any good," Evy told him.

"It will, too, when I get through talking to him."

However, I wasn't going to go back on my word. I've always contended that, had I flown directly into Iowa City from Kansas City, I would not have taken the Oregon State job. There were some people waiting there, and I'm sure after I listened to them, I couldn't have afforded to come to Oregon State for $21,000.

I believe one of the reasons I was hired at Oregon State was because I had a long history of relationships with black athletes, dating back to Wichita East days. At the time, Oregon State was having the problems with racial unrest among black athletes that many universities were experiencing.

The problems with blacks at Oregon State didn't bother me, simply because I felt I'd had the experience to deal with race-oriented issues. After I got there, there was no question there was some feeling against the black athlete. There was prejudice there, just as there is in any place that doesn't have a large black population. There were people there who resented black athletes.

Slats Gill and Style

I made the usual pronouncements when I arrived on the scene. "I think it would be advisable to buy tickets early this year," I was quoted, "because in all due respect, they may not be around very long."

I also mentioned in newspaper stories why we had pulled up stakes—the weather and the strife in the athletic program, which I thought might have been adversely affecting recruiting during my last years at Iowa. The Iowa Fieldhouse also had been deteriorating and I was unsure when a move would be made to build a new one. Indeed, Carver-Hawkeye Arena did not open until January, 1983.

Barratt noted my age of 51. We were entering an era when the coaches would be younger and the men of my age were often getting out of coaching. "Why," Barratt said, "he's got at least 14 good years left."

When I got to Oregon, my priority was to hire assistant coaches. Dick Schultz would replace me at Iowa, and Lanny had already departed for Arkansas so I was barefoot for help. One position was taken by Dave Leach, who came from Burlington Junior College. I decided quickly I also wanted to hire Jim Anderson, a former OSU player and assistant coach. Jimmy had reservations. "I don't know," he said. "I don't know anything about the way you play basketball. You certainly don't play like Slats."

Amory "Slats" Gill had coached at Oregon State for 36 years, from 1929-1964, and was a legendary figure around OSU. His calling cards were ball-control and defense, and Valenti had sustained those traditions through his years.

"Jimmy, I understand what you're saying," I told him, "but on the other hand, you don't know anything about our basketball, either. There's only one way you're going to find out, and that's to stay with us. At the end of your first year, you'll find out there's basically no difference in what I do on the basketball floor and the way Slats Gill did it, except that we approach the game from different angles."

> Jim Anderson: "The first couple of weeks after Paul Valenti resigned, I knew what my chances were. Paul was very instrumental in the hiring process, going out and interviewing, and Jim Barratt very definitely had it in his mind right from the start he wasn't going to hire me, and Paul told me that.
>
> "One time, when I was working for Paul maybe six years prior, I asked him who people in the profession feel are the great coaches. And he said, there's a guy Slats Gill thought was one of the up-and-coming coaches—Ralph Miller at Iowa. I never knew him at Wichita or Iowa, but if I hear it from Slats and I hear it from Paul, it must be true.
>
> "I thought about leaving, but you know my background and my love for Oregon State. When Ralph asked me, I was flattered. He asked me over the phone. I had never met him, didn't even know what he looked like. From the start, he was great, no phoniness, no B.S., he said it the way it was. We talked about my philosophy, whether I could fit in with his philosophy, and it's amazing, we came out so unbelievably close it was almost scary. The styles were different, but in what you want out of your athletes, how you pass, cut, how you play defense, it was all the same."

During my college days at Kansas University.

Jean and me with our children Susan and Cappy at the time of my hiring at Wichita University.

From left to right—me, Tony Lockyear, Dale Skelton, Phog Allen. Three men who helped shape my career.

Gary Thompson and me with two young boys during a summer basketball camp.

Taking it easy during one of the thousand-
plus games of my coaching career.

A reunion of the great 1954 Wichita team.

The 1969-70 Iowa team—undefeated Big Ten Champions.

The 1980-81 Oregon State team—Pac-10 champions.

The 1981-82 Oregon State team—Pac-10 Champions.

My last team.
The 1988-89
Oregon State
club.

Dave Leach,
captain of the 1965
Wichita State team
and my former
assistant at
Oregon State.

Me with long-
time friends and
assistant
coaches Jim
Anderson, left,
and Lanny Van
Eman, right.

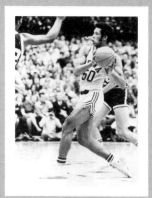

One of the leaders on the great 1970 Iowa team, John Johnson.

Former Iowa great "Downtown" Fred Brown.

All-American at Wichita in 1963, Dave Stallworth.

The star of my final teams, Gary Payton.

Leader of the 1981 Pac-10 champions, Steve Johnson.

Oregon State and NBA great, A.C. Green.

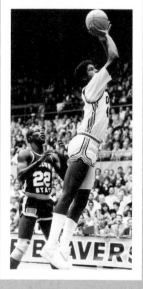

The court at Gill Coliseum,
named in my honor.

Television screen showing our 1981
victory over UCLA—OSU's first victory
at Pauley Pavilion.

Celebrating our win to clinch the 1980 Pac-10 title.

Hands-Off Recruiting

I feel I've always been blessed, not only in having good assistant coaches, but in having them a long time. There were never any personality clashes, any power struggles, anything that disrupted the program or the process. I had only nine assistant coaches in 41 years of coaching.

At East, I had Frank Henkel. In college, I started with my brother Dick, who was with me at Wichita before being named assistant athletic director there. Then I had Brice Durbin, who was with me just a year before hooking up with the Kansas High School Activities Association, and is now executive secretary for the National High School Athletic and Activities Association. Then there was Gary Thompson, who had played for me at East and Wichita, and after military service, returned to coach for me when Dick went into administration.

Lanny Van Eman was there briefly with me at Wichita and followed me to Iowa. At Iowa I retained Dick Schultz, who was the assistant under Sharm Scheuerman. At Oregon State there were Dave Leach, Jimmy Anderson, and Lanny again when Dave took the Boise State job. Finally, Freddie Boyd for my final two years at OSU. Jimmy Anderson was with me the entire 19-year tenure at Oregon State, and he was a wonderful friend, a great assistant and he's now a fine head coach.

Nine assistants, and they were all great. I always felt my time belonged to the players, not to recruiting, and that they'd gain much more with me there. What evolved was a system in which, essentially, my assistants told me who to recruit. Throughout the years, my assistants have done a great job finding players who could play the pressure system..

Lanny Van Eman: "Ralph got burned by recruiting at times. There was one player who said he was coming to Wichita and didn't show up. As the recruiting thing started to get a little more scurrilous, my impression was, Ralph wanted nothing to do with it.

"In any case, the musician Herb Alpert was sweeping the nation one year while we were at Iowa, and he was coming to Iowa on a tour. I had

a friend who could get us six tickets, front and center, so I asked Ralph, 'Are you interested in Herb Alpert on Friday?'

And he says, 'OK, who's Herb Alpert, what position does he play? I know you've told me about him.'

"I backed off and asked Jean, and she was duly excited about it, and she dragged Ralph out to see Herb Alpert. But that was his approach, in great measure, to recruiting."

Tragedy at Oregon State

My first year at Oregon State will always be remembered less for my arrival than for tragedy.

Paul had bequeathed me a pretty fair group, actually. Freddie Boyd, now coaching for Jimmy at OSU, was a junior guard, and the leading scorer on that team at 17.8 points a game. Freddie was quick, fast, an excellent athlete who was perfectly suited for our system. He would spend seven seasons in the NBA.

Freddie was the start of our Bakersfield connection. He came to us at the same time as Billy Nickleberry, a popular, effervescent guard from Portland. Billy Nick was really a hit with the fans, but there was no question who the best player was. Well, Freddie was hesitant about usurping Billy Nick, and we had to have a conversation about the situation soon after I came here. One of the things the 76ers didn't like about Freddie after they took him was that he wouldn't shoot enough. He'd never thought about taking that many shots before.

Insofar as the system would allow, Freddie always would take the No. 1 guard on the other team defensively. His greatest ability, I always thought, was to be going as fast as he could—and that was fast—take a jump stop, never lose his balance and go straight up in the air for his jump shot. He was just a good, solid all-around player. Then Dave Leach had brought along Sam Whitehead from Burlington. Sam was a 6'6" forward from Cleveland who led us in rebounding for three straight years.

Our postman was Neal Jurgenson, from an athletic family down the road in Eugene. I remember in speaking with Jimmy about our talent, he said, "Ralph, we've never fast-broken before in our lives. There isn't anybody out there who knows how to fast-break. Personally, I think we're kind of slow. We only have one postman who can move at all, and I don't know if he can fast-break or not."

Well, Jurgy had just never run before. Once he found out that if he got down to the other end in a hurry he might get some easy buckets, he was like a March hare.

Gary Arbelbide, a 6' 7" forward, also started for us, as did Tim Perkins, a 6' 5" guard. Billy Nickleberry was quick and fast and played extensively. Larry Webber was a forward off the bench.

Then there was Mike Keck from Klamath Falls. He was a great athlete in football, basketball, and baseball. I didn't have him when I first got to Oregon State. He had participated in all three sports his freshman year, but by his sophomore year—my first year —he had opted to concentrate on baseball. He was a great pitcher.

He didn't come out for basketball right away. Two weeks after practice started, about the first of November, he walked into my office, introduced himself, told me his dad Al had coached him at Klamath Falls and said they had used pressure defense.

"I think I could play for you," he told me. "I'd like to come out."

"Be my guest," I said. It was tongue-in-cheek because Mike was only about 6' 1" and looked a lot more like a football player than a basketball player. Well, he came out, and it didn't take long for me to figure out that I would play this guy. So he started in our first game.

We came right out of the blocks, beating Oklahoma State a pair at Corvallis and in Portland. We added easy wins over Utah and Brigham Young, both times scoring in the 90s. That was something of an occasion in Corvallis. Paul's teams, playing the close-to-the-vest style of Slats Gill, had scored into the 90s only three times in six years.

We got our come-uppance at Kentucky and Tennessee, but we generally continued to play above expectations. We swept to three straight victories in the Far West Classic, beating a good Oregon team, 68-64, in the first of five meetings with the Ducks that year. We wouldn't beat them again that season, however.

Into January now, we split four conference games and then won a non-league game against Long Island. On the final weekend of the month, we were off. I believe it was customary at that time for the conference schools to be idle or play non-league games because of a couple of league members who were on the semester system and in final exams. So we decided to let our players off for the weekend. They could come in fresh on Monday for the following weekend when we had back-to-back games with Oregon.

Early that Saturday morning, I got the numbing news: Mike Keck had been killed and Larry Webber badly injured in an accident in northern California. They were driving to Reno to spend the weekend.

Larry Webber: "Just on the spur of the moment, Mike asked me if I wanted to go down to Reno. He lived in Klamath Falls, and we were going to just sneak by and see his parents. We'd been drinking at the time. We didn't drink that much, but enough to be impaired, I'm sure. When we got to Klamath Falls, Mike took over the wheel. It was Mike's fraternity brother's car, a Toyota Corolla, and the frat brother was in the back seat. I consumed a lot more than they did.

"We were on a real curvy road, Route 395 outside of Susanville, near the town of Litchfield. I was asleep. Mike had gotten off to the shoulder of the road, over-corrected, went onto the other shoulder, took about 100 feet of barbed-wire fence with him and the car flipped about six times. They don't know if he fell asleep. I was thrown from the car, and apparently it rolled over Mike and crushed him.

"I woke up after the accident. I don't know how long afterwards. I can remember the lights in the car being on. Somehow, I crawled back into the car. I can remember a body being inside the car, this friend of Mike's, who wasn't badly injured. It was really cold. I didn't have a jacket

on or anything. I remember this body shaking. I didn't know if it was dead or alive."

Early that week, when we should have been upbeat over our start and refreshed from a break in mid-season, we were attending Mike's funeral and mourning his loss.

I suspect it was more physical than psychological, but our season suddenly went south. Before the accident, I had really felt we had six players, and now we had four. At 10-4 before the accident, we immediately went on an eight-game losing streak. It didn't end until we swept the Washington schools at our place late in the season.

I was very proud of that team because we were in the thick of many games, even though we were totally outmanned. They played their hearts out. But our games with Oregon, five of them, captured the importance of Mike and Larry to our team. With them for one game, we won. Without them the other four, we lost each one. We finished 12-14.

The next year we were 18-10, and at 9-5, third in the Pac-8. Freddie averaged just under 20 points a game to lead us, and in Mike's absence, we usually started a popular guard from the little central Oregon town of Madras, Ron Jones.

The accident cost us not only that first year, but really, for at least another two years. Mike had only been a sophomore when he was killed. Larry was a junior, of course, did not play anymore the rest of the 1970-1971 season, but did try, after grueling work, to play his senior year. But he was never able to play well again.

Larry Webber: "I had run the mile in 5:21 in pre-season conditioning before the accident. I ran 7:21 the next year. At the time of the accident, I weighed 225 and was in the best condition of my life. After six weeks in the hospital, I was released at 160 pounds, nothing but skin and bones.

"During the accident, I severed four lateral ligaments and tore cartilage, ruptured the me-

dial capsule in the knee. They did a real nice job sewing those ligaments up. They couldn't get the knee to work again. Couldn't get movement. So I had a manipulation. They put me out, put these sandbags on my instep and forced the knee down in a downward motion to stretch the ligaments. When I woke up, my knee was the size of a basketball. The doctor came in, put a syringe in it, and fluid and blood came gushing out.

"There were some tough times in the hospital. I had suffered a severe contusion in my chest in addition to the knee. They had to withdraw fluid in there so I have a big nine-inch scar on my left side, where they had to go in and remove a blood clot. Thank God for Ralph. My internist thought that if I hadn't been in the condition I was in, I probably wouldn't have made it.

"I basically made the team that next year because I was a fifth-year senior. It was more for inspiration than anything else. I never had the lateral movement I once had. It was really frustrating, to always be trailing on the break."

12

Lonnie's Legacy

There was nothing too remarkable about the year 1972-1973. We did manage to recruit an exceptional shooter out of San Luis Obispo, California, named Paul Miller, and now that freshmen were again eligible to play, he did. When Paul used to wind up a 25-foot jump shot, he would say he could hear me behind him, rasping, "Better make it."

Usually he would. He would have been devastating with the three-point line.

We also introduced a gifted sophomore guard, Charlie Neal, who would start for us for three years. With Freddie gone to the pros, Sam Whitehead led us in both scoring and rebounding. Down the stretch, we were given a shot at making the National Invitation Tournament (NIT), but lost six of our last seven and finished 15-11.

Recruiting: Ups and Downs

The year 1973-1974 was not a bountiful one—we would go 13-13 and take fifth in the Pac-8 with a 6-8 record—but it was eventful, any way you looked at it.

Let's begin well before that season ever got started. During the winter of 1973, there was a prospect coming out of Portland who was drawing more attention than any player in the history of the state of Oregon. His name was Richard Washington. He played at Benson Tech and was touted all through his high school career to be seven feet tall. Never mind that he was really about 6' 10".

The legend that grew up around Richard not only had him to be that magical height of seven feet, but a shot-blocker as well. He was seen to be that rare, dominating-center type that could put a college program at the forefront for the duration of his stay.

At one time, it looked pretty good for us. Richard had a sister who had already enrolled at Oregon State. His coach, Dick Gray, was an Oregon State alum, and we were recruiting Richard as well as another 6' 6" Benson prospect named Rickey Lee. Well, as it turned out, we came in second to the lures of UCLA.

It wasn't long after he got to Westwood that John Wooden pronounced that Richard wasn't really seven feet, but 6'10". Many people took that as John protecting Richard, setting himself up to look good, but it was true, he was closer to 6' 10". Rather than a dominating center, Richard's real role, both at UCLA, and in the pros, was that of big forward, facing the basket. He was MVP in the national championship game of 1975, John's last year, but he wouldn't be the meal-ticket, postman type that people had mistakenly envisioned. He was a fine player nevertheless.

Meanwhile, in the final days of Washington's recruitment, Gray would come out blasting the University of Oregon's approach with Washington as "bottom of the barrel." Whether that had any effect on Oregon's future outlook about Portland recruiting, I can't say, but this much is true: Oregon didn't have any significant success in the Portland area for another decade, and that would prove to be a boon to us.

Recruiting is a funny business. While the recruiting of Washington was going on—a highly publicized process, every step closely chronicled—we were unobtrusively making hay with an unknown player in California. Lonnie Shelton was a great athlete, no ifs, ands, or questions about it. He was considered to be one of the very top tight end prospects in the country, and ranked highly in the shot put and discus. He had come by his size early, and was reputed to have been about 6' 7" and 220 pounds or so in junior high school, which must have been an imposing proposition for defensive backs at that level.

The first time I saw Lonnie, Buzz Caffee, his high school coach in Bakersfield, had brought him to one of our games in Los Angeles. All these other sports were brought up, and he said, "Coach, I don't want to play football in college. I want to play basketball."

Later, one of the major excuses we heard from coaches after they found out he could play basketball was, "Well, we thought he was going to be a football player."

I always chuckled. We live clear up in Oregon, but when the kid was a sophomore in high school, I knew he wanted to be a basketball player. Lonnie said that John Wooden would have given him a scholarship for basketball, but he wasn't that high on UCLA's list. He had visited USC on a football trip and John McKay had told him he could try out for basketball if football didn't work out, but Lonnie said he wasn't sure he'd get the opportunity. It was the same story at other schools.

True, Lonnie was not a great high school basketball player. The potential was there, but he was just another strong 6' 7" player at that time. But what potential. He's one of the fastest, quickest players I've ever seen. I've always said I never knew a player with quicker hands than Lonnie Shelton. He could strip a 5' 10" guard of the ball in the middle of the court, take it right away from him. Unfortunately, he got called for many fouls because none of the officials believed he could do it. He could take it away, clean as a whistle, and not touch you.

We had a squad meeting one time in September of his freshman year. It was hot in our dressing room, no air conditioning. There was a fly buzzing around Rickey Lee's head in front of Lonnie. So Lonnie was sitting there, watching this fly, and next thing I knew, with a thumb and a forefinger, he caught the fly. I couldn't believe what I saw. Never in my life did I see anybody catch a fly like that, but Lonnie did.

After he had signed with us, Lonnie was participating in some sort of marathon basketball game to raise money at his high school and Jimmy Anderson was making a visit down in Bakersfield. This was just pick-up basketball. Jimmy got back home and said, "Ralph, you know, we really have a basketball player. I never saw Lonnie do what he did today."

UCLA's Weekend Upset

With Lonnie, we parlayed Rickey Lee plus a spindly, sinister-looking 6' 4" guard named George Tucker and a good all-around 6' 7" forward, Don Smith, into an exceptional recruiting class that year. Smith, another catch from Bakersfield, had actually been eligible at the previous mid-season but sat out until fall.

We wouldn't click right away, losing three of four on a difficult opening road trip to the East. We did come back and turn some heads in the semifinals of the Far West Classic, where Oregon State has played consistently well for years.

We faced Bob Knight's ranked Indiana team, with many of the parts of the 1976 undefeated national championship club that some consider the best in the history of the game. This one included Quinn Buckner, Kent Benson, Scott May, Bob Wilkerson, and Steve Green. In the first game of the tournament, Indiana simply dismantled Brigham Young by about 40 points.

We did a great job controlling the tempo. Charlie Neal committed ten of our 17 turnovers, but he had nine assists and led us with 15 points against the grinding pressure of Buckner. We won, 61-48. We got beat the next night for the title by Washington.

February brought one of the most memorable weekends in the history of Oregon sports. We hadn't played consistently since the Indiana upset, losing six of ten games. We were coming off a pair of games in Los Angeles in which we had lost respectably to USC and UCLA. John Wooden's team came to Corvallis with a 50-game winning streak in Pac-8 games. This was the senior year of the Walton Gang, and it was considered almost unbeatable. The previous year UCLA had thrashed Memphis State in the national finals when Walton had his unforgettable 21-for-22 night and scored 44 points.

With a team seemingly too young to be cowed, we hung with UCLA. Doug Oxsen, our 6' 10" junior center, did a marvelous job beating Walton to spots. As we usually managed to do, we kept the Bruins from getting off on their fast-break. In the final 30 seconds, Tucker dropped in four straight free throws, and we came up 61-57 winners, ending that long, long UCLA streak that carried over three and a half years of conference play.

As luck would have it, Dick Harter had a pretty fair ball club at Oregon, too. In those days, we were playing back-to-back games. So, no more than 16 or 17 hours after losing to us, UCLA was playing an afternoon TV game in Eugene, and lost to the Ducks—two conference losses for UCLA in the span of less than 20 hours when it hadn't lost for 50 games before then. Well, between us, we sent *Sports Illustrated* scrambling. The cover the next week headlined, "UCLA's Lost Weekend." But somehow, in the writeup, you didn't even know we were the ones that broke the streak. Our game was just forgotten. It turned into a story on Oregon's rebuilding under Dick Harter. Yes, it did smart a little, but then, somebody pointed out that the author was Kenny Moore, an Oregon graduate.

The weekend's activity wasn't over. USC was the team that really made out that weekend, beating both Oregon and us. In the course of our game that Saturday night with USC, I got to take the long walk from our bench to the exits. I was ejected for three technical fouls, the second and final ejection of my career.

My argument was really with Jack Ditty, the official. I got one technical talking to him, but then Mel Ross later gave me a second. Still later he gave me a third. I always contended I deserved the first one, but not the last two.

Just another weekend in the life of a college basketball coach.

An Explosive Rivalry

Our season seemed headed for an innocent ending at our place against Oregon. We had had a spotty year typical of a young team—some exhilarating highs, but certainly a lot of disappointment along with it. Against the Ducks, we took a big lead, and in fact, had the game pretty much wrapped up by halftime. But Oregon made a run at us, and with just a few seconds left, we were still several points ahead. Then there was a stoppage of play.

In those days, we had the Chancellor's Trophy, emblematic of state supremacy in basketball. And so, with a few seconds left, one of our male cheerleaders, Rick Coutin, was given the trophy — which would be in our possession for a year, with our winning two of three that season — and he ran along the perimeter of the court, holding the trophy high for our fans. Well, in a moment of pique, Dick Harter stuck out his leg and tripped Rick Coutin, sending Rick sprawling and the trophy flying. It got a pretty good dent in it.

Before the game was over, Dick asked at the scorer's table whether there was a way for his team to leave the floor without making the usual diagonal exit, which was a wise move. The

Ducks did so and we avoided any further problems. Shortly after that, we retired the concept of the Chancellor's Trophy, dent and all. It was the best thing Dick and I ever did.

When I first came to Oregon State, we were playing two non-league games with the Ducks in mid-season. Then, if we ended up playing them in Portland at the Far West Classic—as we did in 1970-1971—we had the potential to play them five times in a season. That's a bit much.

When Dick came to Oregon, we agreed we had to do something about the Chancellor's Trophy. We didn't like it for one important reason: You were establishing a state champion, rather than a Pac-8 champion, and both of us were interested in much more than being state champion. Gradually, we were able to do away with the non-league games. In 1972-1973, Dick's second year at Oregon and my third at OSU, we cut back to one non-league game between us, played in Portland. In 1978-1979, the year after he left for Penn State, we did away entirely with the third game, which was all to the good.

The furor that accompanied the dent in the trophy was only typical of the Oregon-Oregon State rivalry in those days. That rivalry is hard to describe. It seemed as though everything possible happened for a few years. I have never seen, anywhere, any rivalry as intense as the one between Oregon and Oregon State. It was the fans. I think many people were under the impression that Dick and I shared a great animosity. Nothing could have been further from the truth. We had a professional respect, and liked each other.

We did have some gnawing, memorable battles. In Dick's very first year at Oregon, the Ducks went winless in Pacific-8 play, and we had an unfortunate incident as the season finale wound down in our gym. During a timeout, one of our male cheerleaders was given the public-address microphone—ill-advisedly—and he said, "We'd like to congratulate Oregon on being the first team in Pac-8 history to go 0-14."

In the first game after the tripping incident, at our place in 1975, we were a point down in overtime with five seconds left and the ball out underneath our basket. We got the ball in the corner to a forward named Roosevelt Daniel, but Oregon had him trapped. So he flung it out to Rickey Lee, and from 30 feet or more, he jackknifed his body, hurled a shot, and at the buzzer, it banked in to give us a 72-71 victory.

Then in the last game of that regular season at Eugene, we played a dandy game, tied at 80 down the stretch. Oregon took a last shot, missed, but Greg Ballard tipped the ball in and Oregon won. The *Eugene Register-Guard* the next day showed a picture of the light on behind the basket standard as the ball was in Ballard's hand—signifying that time had run out—a fact I attempted to bring to the attention of Mel Ross just after it occurred. But Mr. Ross was quicker off the floor than I was, so my complaint went unheeded.

There were bench-clearing incidents. There was a fever pitch to the games. And there were great athletes, Ballard and Ronnie Lee playing for Oregon, and Lonnie and others for us. In the 1976 game in Portland, we were six behind with a minute to play in regulation when Lonnie made some great athletic plays to bring us even before we lost in overtime. There was just an electricity to those games. After Dick left Oregon, we more or less got in command of the state. Dick and I had played our series pretty evenly, but in recent years, Oregon State has things its own way, winning 15 in a row at one stretch and 24 of the last 26.

Turning it Around

Finally, in 1975, we made a breakthrough. Until that year, teams other than conference champions had to content themselves by attending the NIT, if they were good enough. The NCAA was only taking conference winners, and there were some pretty graphic examples of justice miscarried. USC, in 1970-1971, was probably the most prominent, losing only two games during the regular season to UCLA. And it couldn't go to the NCAA.

We would be the first from the Pac-10 to make the NCAAs as an at-large entry. We got off to a good start at 5-0 before losing at North Carolina State, the defending national champion. Then we slid a bit, losing four straight, the last a one-point game at Nevada-Reno.

A few players would point to that night as the one when we turned it around. Some of our kids thought they shouldn't pass up the pleasures of Reno after our game, so they came in after curfew. I was up waiting for them, and had some choice words about what direction we were heading.

I guess I got their attention. We split with the Bay Area schools at home the following weekend, but then took off, winning nine of our next 11 conference games and losing only to UCLA in two competitive games. We had back-to-back victories against a very good USC team led by Gus Williams and Clint Chapman, including one at home when Lonnie had 27 points, seven rebounds, seven assists, and seven blocked shots. In the very next game against USC, Lonnie had 25 points and 14 rebounds. He was coming of age.

Back then NCAA bids were awarded even before the regular season was over, and before our finale with Oregon, we happily accepted a invitation to the Mideast Regional at Lexington against Middle Tennessee State.

We advanced without much trouble against Middle Tennessee. Then, because we were playing five days later just up the road at Dayton, we stayed back there. The joy ride ended against Indiana, top-ranked and mature since our Far West Classic victory the previous year. George Tucker missed a layup on our first possession, which was to be indicative of our night. Lonnie got in foul trouble, played only about 11 minutes, and we fell behind by 21 at halftime before losing 81-71. Then we lost to Central Michigan in a consolation game that prevented us from a 20-win season. Once again, foul trouble dogged Lonnie; he had only 13 minutes. We certainly didn't get the best of it back there. Lonnie played only 24 minutes in two games. We ended the year at 19-12.

A Lost Season

The off-season was almost as eventful as the season had been. The 1975-1976 season figured to be an excellent one for us. Tucker, Shelton, and Don Smith would be juniors, all with vast experience, Paul Miller was a senior, and we added a terrific shooter from Butte Junior College, Rocky Smith.

Instead, it would be a tumultuous year because of events that began in June. Shortly after students had left for the summer, we got an important call from Buzz Caffee, Lonnie's high school coach. Seems that Lonnie had called him from Cincinnati, saying a couple of agents had talked him into going back there and exploring the possibility of signing with the old American Basketball Association.

They were the Delpit brothers. I hope they're not agents anymore, but they were in business long enough to cause us many problems. Buzz said he was leaving Bakersfield in an hour or so, and did I know anything about this? I didn't. I don't think there was any consideration whatsoever on Lonnie's part about going pro at that time. Nobody in those days signed a pro contract after his sophomore year.

Lonnie Shelton: "The St. Louis team had sent a couple of agents out here to talk me into going pro. They came to my house and said they'd like for me to come back and just be there when the draft is going on. I flew back with them. I didn't know the NCAA rules and stuff. I didn't know I was losing my eligibility by doing it.

"I didn't even get to pack. They had just flown me away without a bag. We went first to Cincinnati. There was another agent there, Ron Grinker. They made an attempt to fly my high school coach, Buzz Caffee, out, but they had him flown somewhere else where he couldn't get there to advise me. After I got there, they said they wanted me to go to St. Louis, and talk about a contract. They flew Buzz to Cincinnati, when they knew I was going to be in St. Louis.

"We flew to St. Louis that night. I went out with Marvin Barnes (then with the St. Louis Spirits) in his Rolls-Royce with a telephone in it. We went to a club and had a couple of drinks. Then we went back up to the hotel after midnight, and they had me reading a contract, trying to understand all this legal stuff, pressuring me to sign a contract. They had lawyers there, Harry Weltman (now senior vice president and gen-

eral manager of the New Jersey Nets) was there. He was general manager of the team. It was all them against me.

"I signed at three a.m. The next morning, Buzz Caffee showed up, and I told him what happened. We took the contract to a lawyer in St. Louis to evaluate it. It was one million dollars, spread out over 12 years. There were a lot of clauses that, if I didn't perform, they could void the contract."

Lonnie was hot-boxed real good. He succumbed to the pressure, but he never cashed that $5,000 bonus check. Almost immediately after signing, he began his appeal to be reinstated. It was denied by the NCAA, and I was disappointed they didn't view his situation with a little humanity. My view was that this was a real hot-box situation where he had no guidance. It went to the courts. A Portland firm took over his lawsuit. There was no question Lonnie was going to be a pro and make big money, and his arrangement with the attorney was on a contingency basis.

In November, Lonnie won an injunction against the NCAA in the U.S. District Court of Portland Judge Gus Solomon, allowing him to be back with us for the 1975-1976 season, but only amid much controversy. Among others, Marv Harshman at Washington was extremely outspoken in saying the whole affair was wrong.

I kind of resented Marv's attitude. I felt the NCAA had a great opportunity with Lonnie's case to spike a few of the more unscrupulous agents, but they chose not to. Marv was stuck on the fact the rule was broken, and didn't want to look at the circumstances involved. The damage was done, but Lonnie never cashed that check. If he was a pro because of signing something under those circumstances, I'll never understand it.

There were also many people who wanted us not to play Lonnie after all this. But technically, the lawsuit was against the NCAA and Oregon State. When the courts ruled in favor of Lonnie, there was no choice in the matter.

It wasn't a year easily forgotten. The Shelton affair grew to gain even more publicity because we began the conference season 4-0. Included among the four was a resounding win over UCLA in Corvallis, which Lonnie had punctuated with a resounding slam-dunk near the final buzzer. The dunk, of course, was still illegal in college basketball at this time so it cost us a technical foul—but it did please the crowd immensely.

We lost to Oregon and California, but followed with three straight conference victories. We were 7-2 and very much challenging UCLA's dominance when we went to meet the Bruins in Los Angeles. We took them to the wire before losing 78-69. In 30 minutes before fouling out in the late going, Lonnie had 24 points, 11 rebounds, and five assists. I still contend that the fifth foul should have gone to Paul Miller; Lonnie was 10 feet from the action when it was called.

Late the next morning, Lonnie was getting a snack at the hotel and we were an hour or so from getting on a bus to the Sports Arena to practice for a Saturday afternoon game with USC. Then we got the news.

A three-judge panel from the Ninth Circuit U.S. Court of Appeals in Seattle had ruled in favor of the NCAA. Lonnie had played his last game for us.

"It is not judicial business to tell a voluntary athletic association how to play its games," said Judge Eugene A. Wright.

Our last four games that season were among my most satisfying as a coach. With 24 hours to ponder how to fill in for Lonnie, we blew away USC, 80-61, using Tim Hennessey as a 6' 5" high-post player. Then we came home for our final three. We beat Washington State with no trouble, upset Marv Harshman's Top Ten-ranked and NCAA-bound Washington team 73-64, and ended it all with a one-point loss to Oregon.

We finished 18-9, but there was no NCAA invitation—no surprise there. Lonnie's legacy was three straight years of leading us in scoring and rebounding, and a notation in the NCAA record books that shows us having forfeited the 15 victories in which he participated during his final season.

13

Replacing a Legend

In retrospect, I made some faulty assumptions before accepting the job at Oregon State. My personal creed is that replacing a legend, at the time of his retirement or death, is not a good move, regardless of the opportunity involved. Since my early years, I have known and been associated with legends such as Dr. Allen and Henry Iba, and have been aware of the problems of those who replace them.

Slats Gill was truly a legend at Oregon State, a man who began coaching at OSU in 1929 and won 599 games in 36 years. I knew him personally and respected him as a man and coach.

My experience at Iowa had lulled me to sleep because the situation was almost identical to Oregon State. Bucky O'Connor, a personal friend, took Iowa to the national finals in 1956 with the Fabulous Five, but was killed in an auto accident in 1958, so he didn't live long enough to become a true legend. His replacement, Sharm Scheuerman, coached for six years, and after his tenure, there were no comparisons made between Bucky and me. Because of the similarities between OSU and Iowa, I made the mistake of assuming that enough time had elapsed after Slats' retirement that comparisons would be minimal.

Of Legends . . .

My first three years at Oregon State was a difficult period. The tragic auto accident involving Mike Keck affected the progress of the program for that year and the next two. Meanwhile, I was surprised to learn that our efforts were not being compared to Paul Valenti's, but rather, to Slats' by most of the fans.

We won 19 games in the season of 1974-1975, and our second-place finish in the Pac-8 was good enough for a trip to the Mideast Regional of the NCAA tournament. We followed with 18 wins the next year. The improvement in the won-loss record, however, did not greatly improve the coach-fan relationship in some quarters, which, of course, bruised my ego.

Our first exhibition game following my arrival at Oregon State was in the little town of Harrisburg. One of the local writers covered the game. After it was over, he asked people in the stands what they had thought of the game.

"I think Coach Miller has set the game back 50 years," said one man.

Well, I had thought I was pretty well up on the scene, but there were many people who had to be convinced I was capable of coaching.

There was a breach of understanding. Fans didn't appreciate my self-assuredness. From their standpoint, Oregon State had had a rich basketball tradition; it was the third school, behind Kansas and Kentucky, to surpass 1,000 victories. There were people who didn't think I understood that. Darrell Aune, our radio play-by-play man, asked me a question one time on the air that year, and I responded with, "Well, that's a stupid question."

At the same time, I didn't see why the fans didn't appreciate a new, and winning, style of basketball. It was a cold war. I don't recall hearing much flak directly, but I was aware of it. Jimmy Anderson had been around a good many years and he would let me in on a few of the comments from time to time.

With these attitudes as a backdrop, you have the reality of my first several years at Oregon State. Through Lonnie Shelton's departure, we had had essentially two waves of teams. The potential of the first was cut short by the accident that killed Mike Keck. The second was never seen to fruition because of the Shelton signing incident. So in discussing the broad picture, I made note of both those misfortunes. I'm sure some people took this rationale as an excuse.

There were also occasional problems with the athletic administration. If I'd had a good job offer elsewhere, I'd have probably taken it. At one point in the mid-1970s, I met with a representative of Clemson University, but their coaching vacancy was filled by Bill Foster.

Jim Anderson: "First of all, here is a person with great credentials coming in. And he has an ego. He's been around, been successful wherever he's been. When he first came in, it was kind of like Oregon State had never had basketball before. It wasn't that he disrespected Slats or Paul, it was, 'I'm coming to town, I'm going to teach you basketball.'

"It kind of took people back a little bit. I think Jim Barratt misled him. I think he gave him the feeling things were down and negative, that he had to come into a situation and pick it up, make people feel good about basketball.

"I stuck up for Ralph, and it wasn't like I stuck up for him because I'm working for him, it was because he was working hard and trying to do the right things. Ralph hasn't treated me to a bad day in my life. I was loyal to him until the last moment.

"It was kind of like Ralph was an outsider for an awful long period of time. He even thought one time of getting out of it. I remember us sitting in a lounge in our hotel in Dayton at the regional in 1975, having a Bloody Mary, and he said to me, 'I think I'm going to hang it up.'

"He had some retirement and a house. Jim Barratt was researching the scene behind Ralph, trying to figure out how much unrest coach was in this faction, testing the water to see how uneasy the general feeling was, and it got back to Ralph. (Now) Barratt always takes all the credit for hiring Ralph.

"That was a very depressing period in Ralph's life, where he was really questioning his situation. That's the first time I'd ever had a talk with Ralph where I was getting after him:

You're a great coach, what the hell's the matter with you? Go down fighting.

"To me, the time when he was first really accepted, when they said, 'We appreciate you, we understand, we love you now,' was when we had those problems with Lonnie and we still rallied around and won. All of a sudden, people said, 'Ralph, you did a hell of a job.'

To me, that was a turning point in the respectability, both ways. The whole thing kind of flip-flopped."

Jean Miller: "I'm sure there were many times when I felt he was abrupt with boosters, but that's his way. I guess the most important thing is, the ones Ralph worked with over the years are still his best friends.

"Slats was a different ilk of a man. He would coffee klatch with the men in Corvallis, and they felt they were part of the act. Ralph has never been that way.

"Many coaches thrive on the public-relations aspect of coaching. Ralph has never sought nor wanted it."

A Devilishly Quick Man

Our off-the-beaten-track style of recruiting struck again in the off-season following Shelton's departure. Two years prior to this, we had recruited a guard, Leon Jordan, who hailed from San Bernardino, California. Through Leon, and Leon's high school coach, John Powell of San Gorgonio High, we learned the intriguing story of a prospect named Steve Johnson.

Steve was 6' 10", and his family was Seventh Day Adventist. The father was a Korean War veteran, disabled, and was on a pension. Steve and all his siblings attended the Seventh Day Adventist school. Steve had asked his dad if he could attend school at San Gorgonio, but was refused permission. So essentially, he left home in order to be able to play basketball at San Gorgonio in San Bernardino. Well, there was another player at San Gorgonio whom we knew was a senior, and we called John Powell to check on him.

"You know," he said, "I've got a big kid that's never played basketball until this year named Steve Johnson. I think he's better than the one you're looking at. You better come down here and look at him."

We did. Amazingly, not one four-year school in California offered this kid a scholarship. There were three colleges that offered him one — Oregon State, Texas, and Idaho. Sometimes the recruiting process is a complete folly.

Steve was devilishly quick for a big man. Defense has never been his strong suit, but offensively, he was a devastating force. He had a nice hook shot, and, back to the basket, a mean first step along the baseline. He simply overmatched most college defenders.

We got great satisfaction out of pulling that one off. Gene Bartow, the UCLA coach then, said he couldn't understand how somebody could be as good as Steve was, and never get any ink in the *Los Angeles Times*. After his senior year, Steve played in a summer league in Los Angeles and performed impressively. Bob Boyd, then the coach at USC, saw Steve wearing a Texas T-shirt that he had picked up on a visit there.

"Hope you have a great career with Texas," Bob told him.

"Thank you very much, Coach," Steve said, "but I'm not going to Texas."

"Oh. Where are you going to school?"

"Oregon State."

The only rational explanation for Steve's lack of notice is that the recruiting process can exclude prospects who don't blossom until their senior years. Because Steve never played before that, he simply didn't show up on any lists that might have been put together before his senior season. Strange but true.

Steve left an early calling card as a freshman in our home opener against Arizona during the 1976-1977 season. He scored 28 points in a losing effort. But we weren't headed anywhere special that year with Steve still learning the ropes. Although we had a senior-dominated team, it was clear that with Lonnie gone—drafted by the New York Knicks—there was a big void.

We had a memorable non-league game at home just before Christmas, in which we allowed Creighton to hit its first 18 shots against us and we lost by 22 points. Defense was not our best attribute that year. It was an erratic season. We lost our opener in the Far West Classic to Weber State. In a 16-13 year, we closed with a game at Oregon that was much like our season: Sporadic and unpredictable.

We played possibly the poorest seven minutes imaginable at Eugene and fell behind 19-3. But then Rocky Smith, a nerveless shooter, started gunning us back into it. Somehow, at McArthur Court, one of the toughest places to play — straight up, let alone 16 down in the first half — we came back to lead by one at halftime, and when it went to overtime, we survived, 78-73. It was a typical wild and woolly Civil War game. Greg Ballard had 40 points and 15 rebounds for Oregon. Seven players fouled out and there were 68 fouls called. Rocky's 32 points helped win it for us.

The Pivotal Recruiting Season

That recruiting season was perhaps the most pivotal in my tenure at Oregon State. It was one of those rare occasions when the state produces a bumper crop of players. Ironically, they were all big guards, about 6' 4".

Danny Ainge, a high school All-American at North Eugene, headed the list. Then there was Mark Radford at Grant in Portland, Ray Blume at Parkrose, Jeff Stoutt at Lake Oswego, and Bob Fronk at Sunset in Beaverton.

The battle for Ainge was lively. Oregon thought it had him. We thought we were in very good shape. Eventually, Ainge fell in love with Brigham Young and went there. But we didn't do so badly. Oregon put all its eggs in the Ainge basket, leaving us carte blanche on the others. Quietly, on signing day, we took Blume and Stoutt and later, Radford joined the fold. We were never really in it with Fronk, and he went to Washington.

Mark Radford was one of the real smoothies of the game. Everything he did looked easy. He was just a very fluid player and a good athlete, a high jumper at Grant. Stoutt was an exceptional shooter. His quickness was suspect, but he could shoot. Ray Blume had played the post at Parkrose, but we projected him as a guard. He was a rangy player, good shooter and good competitor. Another key addition that year was Bill McShane, a 6' 7" post player from Houston, whose family ties to the state of Oregon helped us land him. Mark started from the get-go, and Stoutt was generally a useful sixth-man type, but Ray had some problems early, not all of his own making.

We had a player named Dwayne Allen, about 6' 4" and 195 pounds. He was probably the worst shooter I ever had, but absolutely one of the best defensive players I've ever seen. He was physical, strong, played belly-to-belly, and because he knew he couldn't contribute much with his scoring—aside from being a very good passer—he was going to make his presence felt with defense. Did he ever. His arms reminded you of a windmill, they never stopped moving.

Well, Dwayne was a sophomore on that team. He would always size up a freshman and say, "That's the only one that could take my position." That year, he picked out Ray. Every time you looked up out there, Dwayne was guarding Ray Blume. Every scrimmage situation, he had him. I think Ray was ready to give up the ship and go home. Dwayne totally frustrated Ray. I finally had to call Ray in and straighten him out.

"Is he quicker or faster than you?" I asked Ray.

"I don't think so," Ray said.

"Is he a better shooter?" Well, there wasn't much doubt about the answer to that question. People used to cheer lustily for Dwayne if he could make a free throw.

"So why don't you admit," I asked Ray, "that he knows how to use his skills better than you do yours?"

That helped. By January, he was starting to pull out of his doldrums.

We also took a fellow named Andy McClouskey from nearby Lebanon. Andy was not very big, about 5' 10", but a great outside shooter. He helped us in spots before a knee injury ended his career, and now he's an excellent assistant coach for Jimmy.

So that was a bountiful recruiting class. Not only did we bring in talent, but we got it within state borders, a matter of great pride to many people.

Injuries and a Remarkable Season

If you scanned our first few scores that year, you would be tempted to conclude that it was going to be a horrendous season. We lost Steve Johnson to a stress fracture of the foot in the preseason, and wouldn't have him until several games into the year.

It wasn't as though we didn't need him. An ambitious schedule took us into North Carolina for two games against Dean Smith's team, and one against a good club at Wake Forest. Then, a couple of days after returning, we had to play Oregon in the last of the annual non-league games with the Ducks.

It was an educational month for us. Boy, did we get taken to school! We lost by 31 at North Carolina, 20 at Wake, and 26 at North Carolina. Then we came home and met Oregon. The Ducks were fired up for this one because we had swept the three games the season before, and our promotions people concocted a poster showing Steve Johnson dunking over one of the Oregon players. We shot an astonishing 25 percent, and they slaughtered us, 78-51.

We got Steve Johnson back from the foot injury, and appeared to be on the road to recovery. Then, in a loss at Boise State just before Christmas, he broke his foot cleanly. This time it was going to keep him out for the season. It was another in a rash of stress fractures that we went through in those years, and I couldn't figure out why. Certainly the shoes were much better than in the past, and our practices hadn't changed. We had an excellent gym floor at Gill Coliseum.

So after Steve came back to us in 1978-1979 off what would be a redshirt year, I conducted a little experiment: The only difference I could see from previous years was that now the dunk was back in the game. I've never been a big fan of the dunk, anyway, but I told him the only time I wanted to see him dunking was when he was able to go up on two feet and come down on two feet. No off-balance dunking, creating any undue pressure on the foot. Whether that was a factor, I don't know, but we never had any problem after that.

It was one of the most rewarding of seasons. After the loss of Steve, we had a team meeting, and I explained that if we were going to be successful, it would require great defense, ball control, and good shot selection. Whereas we might have been a team that scored about 80 points a game with Steve, suddenly we scored in the neighborhood of 60 without him.

Rickey Lee was the senior leader, Bill McShane took over at the post, and Mark Radford and Ray Blume were key players as freshmen. We upset Villanova by one point in the Far West Classic on a short shot by Steve Smith in the final seconds. We went to USC, and in one of the great comebacks I've ever been around, we came from 14 behind well into the second half to take the game into overtime and win. Andy McClouskey hit a couple of big shots in that one for us.

As an indicator of how far we had come from early December to late January, we beat Oregon by 14—in Eugene. We would lose to the Ducks at our place in a close one to end the season, in Dick Harter's last game at Oregon. We had no quarrel with the year — 16-11, 9-5 in the Pac-8 for second place. We had a lot to look forward to.

That season, on our trip to Los Angeles, Al McGuire paid a visit to my hotel room. He was in town to televise a UCLA game the next day and had seen us play the Bruins that night.

"Got a big guy coming back next year," I told Al. "We're going to have a good ball club the next couple of years."

I got a short note after that season was over from Dean Smith, whose North Carolina team had whipped us so badly in the early season.

"Congratulations on your season," it read. "Your kids must have come on real well after you got Johnson back."

Little did he know.

The Marvelous 26-4 Season

I suppose the injury to Steve Johnson served one oblique purpose: It put him in the same eligibility class as Radford and Blume, as well as Stoutt, so they all grew together.

Our 1978-1979 season, like the one before, didn't begin with much promise. We had a terrible time getting to Creighton for our opener because of fog and lost by 14. But we rebounded to win our next seven before running into a Michigan State team in the Far West Classic that had a fellow named Magic Johnson on it. We were competitive against a team that would win the national championship that year, losing 65-57. Magic did something that night that would become pretty common for him in the NBA. He had the so-called "triple-double": 10 points, 10 rebounds, 10 assists.

We were spotty in conference play, however. It was still a young team, with four sophomores playing extensively. We lost a two-pointer at UCLA with a last shot to tie it, and then blew a late lead and fell to USC in overtime. That set the tone for an in-and-out conference season.

After the lost weekend in Los Angeles, we came home and set what still stands as the school scoring record, beating Arizona, 116-80, in its first season in the Pac-10 Conference. But we couldn't establish enough consistency to make a run at the championship. A February trip to Arizona was symbolic of our difficulties. We won big at Arizona, came back two nights later—perhaps after too much fun in the sun—and got whipped badly by Arizona State, allowing a then-conference record 76-percent shooting night by ASU. We lost to Oregon by a point in our regular-season finale, 45-44. That would be the last time for awhile that would happen.

We did, however, get a bid to the NIT. We played an athletic team from Nevada-Reno at home, and had a slim lead inside the final minute. Then a slight, six-foot guard named Michael "Fly" Gray threw in a 25-footer with a few seconds left, got fouled, and converted a three-point play. We were one-point losers, ending at 18-11.

Everything was now in place for a run at the Pac-10 dominance maintained for so long by UCLA. We had the big man, we now had experience, and we had depth. Along the way, we had added a bulky 6' 8" inside player from junior college, named Tony Martin, as well as Rob Holbrook, a rangy 6' 8" shooter from Parkrose, Ray Blume's high school. We hadn't even had to battle for Holbrook. He was a walk-on who blossomed.

We won a couple of easy ones at home and then took three games in Hawaii. The Island ambience almost got us in our first game in Honolulu; we beat Hawaii by a single point. Then we turned it on and won by 30 over the same team the next night.

We came home and got a thorough beating from Jack Avina's

Portland team, which he always had ready for us. But nobody would be beating us for quite awhile.

We beat Oregon on the road to open the conference season in December, then swept to the title in the Far West Classic. On the way, we defeated a Danny Ainge-led Brigham Young club by 15 points, and finally upended a strong Clemson team to win the title.

As the new decade began, we immediately established that UCLA's reign was in jeopardy, forcing 27 turnovers and beating the Bruins at home, 76-67. Blume had 23 points for us, but Stoutt was the real key, hitting nine of 15 off the bench for another 23 points.

The next weekend, we won two tight games on the road against the Arizonas, then returned to sweep the Washington schools. At California the following week, we played so cohesively and efficiently in an 86-55 victory, that one newspaper called it "Clockwork Orange."

At that point, we were 8-0 and the clear favorite to win the title. Playing at Stanford, we ran into an interesting situation. Dick DiBiaso, the coach there, realized he didn't have the guns to stay with us. So he ordered his team into a slowdown game — and those were the days of the weekly televised games in the conference on Monday night. The fans at home were probably bored stiff, but I really never thought twice about it. I've always respected the right to try to play slowdown.

It was one for the books. Stanford was intent on the slowdown right from the start, but we would have been all right if we could have hit anything. As it was, we had a 6-0 lead before Stanford finally scored with just over 10 minutes to go in the half. Then we went stone-cold. We made four of 17 shots in the first half. The score was 12-all at halftime. As it turned out, Dwayne Allen shook loose for the last basket of the game, with exactly 10 minutes remaining. And we won, 18-16.

Ultimately, we ended up holding the ball on them in a move some people questioned because we had the superior talent. I've always believed there aren't too many teams that can control the game any better than my teams could, so we decided to give Stanford a taste of its own medicine. In one possession, we had 97 or 98 passes before we ever took a shot.

A Championship

That was our 14th consecutive victory, giving us a 19-1 record. By this time, we were ranked second in the nation. Rather than return home, we stayed in California that week—well, some of the media frolicked off to Las Vegas—but finally unraveled at UCLA, losing 93-67. We then survived a controversial block-charge call near the finish against USC and won by a point. We were still 10-1 in the league and had five of our final seven at home.

Then came the game that eventually would wrest the championship away from Arizona State and put it in our laps. We were hosting Ned Wulk's team, but we didn't play well. With 1:40 to go, ASU had us down by eight, and Lafayette Lever, the fine guard, was going in for a breakaway. Somehow he missed.

He was all by himself, and all of a sudden, he missed. We got the ball back and that sparked my ball club. Had Lever made the shot, there was no way we were going to come from ten points behind that late.

Well, they proceeded to miss three straight one-and-ones down the stretch, and we took advantage. Finally, Steve Johnson tossed up a little hook shot with nine seconds left. It was goal-tended and we took it to overtime. From there, it was as if we had been given a reprieve. We won 82-75 and had a stranglehold on the conference lead.

We would slip up at Pullman against George Raveling's first NCAA-bound team, but we won out the rest of the way, beating Oregon 67-55 at our place to end the chase. OSU finished at 16-2 in the conference, a game ahead of Arizona State. That near-miss ASU had against us in Corvallis had been the difference.

In 1966, Oregon State had won the Pac-8 championship under Paul Valenti's direction, and there followed years and years of UCLA domination—Lew Alcindor, Bill Walton, Marques Johnson, an 88-game winning streak, and a 98-game home streak. Now another Oregon State team had written an end to that era. When the horn sounded, signaling the finish of the Oregon game, I turned around with my arms in the air and smiled broadly.

Our fun would be short-lived. We were sent to Ogden, Utah, to play the winner of the Weber State-Lamar game in the NCAA tournament. Most observers assumed that Weber, playing at home, would be our opponent. But Lamar, playing a loose, carefree game under Billy Tubbs, beat Weber. Then we fell behind by 16 to Lamar, 32-16, in an absolutely ugly start. We got back within seven at the half, however, and when we tied it shortly into the second half, it appeared we had righted ourselves. We then took several two-point leads but Lamar didn't fold, either.

We were down three just inside the final minute when the clincher came. Mark Radford was called for an offensive foul on what I thought was a questionable call, and I got slapped with a technical. Lamar made one free throw and then came back 15 seconds later with two more and we were behind by six—and dead.

The statistics were pretty shocking. We created only 12 turnovers, far fewer than on our best days. While we had seven more field goals than Lamar, we shot 28 fewer free throws. Steve Johnson had 24 points and 18 rebounds. As the sun set over the Wasatch Mountains that Saturday night in March, we were going home, 81-77 losers. At that moment, it was hard to remind ourselves that we had had a marvelous, 26-4 season.

14

All But Perfect

After the Lamar disappointment, we set about to make a good team great. By some measures, we succeeded.

One of the most familiar recruiting stories to Oregonians is that of Charlie Sitton. Charlie was a farm kid from McMinnville, a gangly 6' 8" postman who led his high school team to a state championship. He was well known in the state even as a freshman because he reached his ultimate height early and because he played for one of the very best prep coaches in Oregon, Nick Robertson.

Two Very Different Players

There were many Sitton family connections with Oregon State, and we were always considered the leaders in the clubhouse with Charlie. He would be one of the very rare blue-chip prospects we could recruit; he was right there in our backyard, 50 miles up Highway 99.

Charlie was not talented in the manner of many top recruits. He wasn't particularly a great jumper and wasn't especially quick or fast. He also needed to add weight to a slight frame. But almost from the time he began playing high school basketball, he was fundamentally very sound, and intelligent. And he could shoot quite well.

Following our Lamar loss, I was headed to the Final Four at Indianapolis, unsure about whether we had Charlie locked up. Washington State, under George Raveling, had made a strong bid, and Notre Dame had been on him. Then word got out that Charlie was going to have a press conference at his high school on the morning of the national semifinals.

In a phone call to Jimmy at halftime of the Purdue-UCLA game, I found out Charlie had picked us. Notre Dame was just too far away for a kid raised on the farm, and while Washington State had appeal for Charlie — it was coming off an NCAA appearance, just as we were — we had everything else he was looking for, and we were much closer. Charlie was a consensus first-team All-America pick, the only real true blue-chip player I've ever signed out of high school.

Our other coveted recruit that year was a completely different type of player. Lester Conner was a 6' 4" kid from the Bay Area who, because of a high school illness, had never really shown much at that level. In fact, he didn't even start at Fremont High School.

However, he went on to two different junior colleges in that area and his abilities were unmistakable. He was a natural talent, lithe, quick, and fast, but his most distinguishing characteristic was smoothness. It was hard to decide between his best two attributes: He could see the floor and pass the ball marvelously; he was also a voracious defender in the passing lanes. In other words, Lester had great court sense.

Lester was also a stylist. That meant that recruiting him wasn't going to be a slam-bang deal. This one would take time. A long time after Charlie had made his decision, Lester was still tarrying over Oregon State and Nevada-Las Vegas. We were easily less glamorous, but still, it was clear he was going to be playing on a gifted team. Lester also knew that we had Ray Blume and Mark Radford returning, and he was wary about entering a situation where the guards were set. Our pitch was that he could play a small forward—or, in reality, what would be a three-guard offense.

His recruitment dragged on and on. Signing date was in early April, but April slipped by and Lester wasn't close to a decision. Most of May was in the books before Lester finally said he was coming.

Now the pieces were in place for a big season. We had Steve Johnson in the middle. He had started for three seasons and even a few games of an aborted fourth. Radford had been a consistent starter for three years, Blume had two years of starting and considerable play as a freshman. We had a couple of excellent shooters off the bench in Jeff Stoutt and Rob Holbrook. In fact, had we had the benefit of the three-point line that season, no telling what we might have accomplished. Blume, Radford, Stoutt, and Holbrook were all deadly from outside, and Johnson kept everybody honest because he was almost unstoppable inside. We had a serviceable backup for Johnson in Bill McShane at 6'7". We knew Sitton and Conner represented immediate help.

The Victory Roll

Our opener was against a very good Brigham Young team at home. It included Danny Ainge, Greg Kite, and Fred Roberts. I had been pondering a dilemma. It was obvious Conner was somebody who could help us immeasurably that year, and being a junior college transfer, he wanted to play early. Meanwhile, Jeff Stoutt was a senior, expecting that the departure of Dwayne Allen would open up playing time for him.

I decided to start Conner against Brigham Young. I figured if he showed everybody he knew the system and could play right away, it would be obvious he was the right choice. He couldn't shoot like Stoutt, but he was clearly more talented all-around. On the other hand, if he had trouble immediately then I would have ammunition to sit him down and bring him along more slowly in December.

Well, Lester was terrible in that game. I played him 15 minutes, and everything you could do wrong, he did. So I sat him down and brought Stoutt off the bench. He hit seven of 11 for 14 points. Blume had 19 points and ten assists and we won, 75-68. Lester would see his shortcomings, come along slowly, and crack the starting line-up after the Far West Classic.

At this point, we were also starting Rob Holbrook, while expecting Sitton to edge him out before too long. We had no trouble with Cal State-Northridge. On the road, we were horrendous defensively against Pepperdine. We trailed by a point with seven minutes left before Johnson took over, and we survived, 82-76. We allowed Pepperdine to shoot 63 percent, but escaped because we shot 62 percent ourselves. In the early part of the season, Johnson's accuracy was phenomenal. He was nine for 12 in this game and would be hitting 79 percent after our first 11 games.

Now 3-0, we started Charlie Sitton against Portland State up at Memorial Coliseum. At the site of some of his best moments, where the Oregon state AAA tournament is held, Charlie didn't disappoint. He was 11 for 11 from the field for 23 points and we romped, 102-58.

Portland was next at our place, the team that had given us our only loss in the first two months of the season the previous year. It wouldn't happen this time, as Johnson went nine for 12 again for 22 points and we shot .623 to win, 92-57.

Our offensive balance was phenomenal at this point. We entered the Far West Classic and Stoutt hit 11 of 14 against Northwestern for 25 points, and we had our fourth straight game topping the .600 mark, at .607. In the semifinals against Rhode Island, we really got clicking. We led 55-23 at halftime and it was over early. Conner was now back in the hunt for a starting position; in this game, he played 32 minutes and had 13 points, eight rebounds, and six assists. He was too good to keep out of there.

Oregon then played a solid game against us, but as usual, we had someone rising to the fore. This time it was Radford and Blume who made the difference, combining for 38 points. I wasn't very happy about 17 turnovers, but we were entering the New Year—and conference play—at 8-0, so I didn't have much to quarrel with.

By now, we were something of a national item. Our big season of 1979-1980, plus an undefeated record entering January, had reinforced that we were one of the stories of that season. For me, it was a mixed blessing. I really enjoyed it, but my obligations doubled or tripled. I've generally been pretty accessible to the press, and I was getting calls from major newspapers in New York, Chicago, and Los Angeles. The wire services would call. I ended up spending a lot of time on the telephone. I would end up reciting old truisms about the 2-2-1, Phog Allen, my 1970 Iowa team and before I knew it, I was on the phone an hour. I can't say I didn't enjoy the publicity, but it was a drain on the schedule.

The first season after I retired from Oregon State, Jimmy Anderson's team was leading the Pac-10, and he told me, "Hey, you forgot to tell me how tough these great seasons are."

I said, "You should have known by now."

We'd come back from road trips at night, and it didn't matter how late it was, there would be 500 or 600 people there to greet us and ask for autographs.

One time, Jean said, "Oh, look at all those people."

Steve Johnson said, not altogether happily, "Yeah, just think of all those fountain pens."

A Grand Time

Our first conference test was at Arizona State. It was an incredibly talented team by any standards. Lafayette Lever and Byron Scott were the guards. Alton Lister played center. The forwards were Johnny Nash and Sam Williams. It wasn't unlike an NBA expansion franchise.

We got an early lead and were up seven at the half, 37-30, but ASU came back and had it tied down the stretch. Inside the five-minute mark, Blume got free for a layup, Radford scored after a steal, and we had a tenuous 63-59 lead. We managed to nurse it in from there even though Johnson fouled out with 1:20 left, and we won by four. McShane played 19 minutes and had nine points.

Arizona was also tough, leading us by two at the half. We were down four early in the second half, but then went on an 11-0 run, with Johnson scoring nine of it from close range and Blume adding a jumper. When Arizona got within two late in the game, Johnson scored five in a 7-0 run and we put it away, 61-49.

Johnson had a 12-for-14 night, and then duplicated it the next game against Stanford. This is what his first 11 games looked like from the field: 7-8, 9-11, 9-12, 8-12, 9-12, 7-9, 6-6, 4-6, 8-11, 12-14 and 12-14.

We were 10-0 and had burst to the second-ranked spot in the country, with DePaul on top. As far as I was concerned, I was more than happy to let Ray Meyer be No. 1.

Next we hosted Stanford. It was no cakewalk with Dick DiBiaso's team within six of us early in the second half. Then

Blume hit two free throws, Radford scored on a jumper, Johnson tipped in Sitton's miss, scored again inside, and Blume stole the ball at midcourt, and laid it in. Timeout, Stanford, after a 10-0 run, and we were on the way to a 76-62 victory.

January 10, 1981, was a special night for Oregon State basketball. First, we showed we could play a little defense. Against a pretty decent California team, with Mark McNamara and Michael Pitts, we burst from a 12-12 tie to a 38-16 halftime lead. Gill Coliseum was rocking. We had 12 steals that night, which led to our shooting .607 on the way to an 80-53 win.

It was during a timeout that a rumor grew to a roar. Darrell Aune announced it over the radio and quickly, the news crackled through the building. High fives were slapped. People hugged. Then they announced it over the public-address system.

DePaul had been upset by Old Dominion. We were going to be No. 1.

I spent much of Monday on the telephone, talking to people in New York and from the wire services. I was wanted on radio talk shows. Oregon State was indeed ranked No. 1 in the nation for the first time in the history of the school.

It seemed as though everybody wanted a piece of us. Memorabilia stands were selling stuff at a record pace, including those silly styrofoam No. 1 fingers. There were basketballs to autograph at the office. Grade-school children came to see us at practice.

I'm told, although I don't remember, that there was a play during the season when we made a steal and went in for a nice fast-break basket. As we were retreating to the other end, Ray Blume was so hyped up that as he ran by the bench he extended his palms to me. I didn't know what to do, so naturally, I slapped hands with him. Here I was, at 61, old enough to be Ray's grandfather, and we're slapping skin over the Orange Express.

It was a grand time for the state of Oregon.

Steve Johnson: "Quite honestly, college was child's play. At the time, we had big games and being ranked No. 1 had its pressures, but it just

doesn't compare to the NBA, with the schedule grinding on you.

"It was fun. It brought the school and the state a lot of notice. Most people thought that if it wasn't UCLA on the West Coast, there wasn't any talent out there. This group of unknowns pulled the focus out there."

The Jaws of Defeat

We had a team to worry about, although it turned out we didn't have much concern in our first game after the ranking came out. Against Oregon at home, we stretched our record to 13-0, creating 18 turnovers in the first half and 30 for the game. Steve Johnson went 10 for 10 for 24 points and we coasted, 82-55.

At Pullman the next week, we got past Washington State without too much trouble, 66-53. It was my 500th victory as a college coach, although I made a point of saying I didn't necessarily consider it a milestone because of the other victories in high school and even in the service. My players didn't heed me. They presented me a brown blazer with a nice inscription on the inside pocket.

George Raveling, the WSU coach, was effusive in his praise of our team: "They remind me of the old New York Knicks, with DeBusschere, Frazier, and Bradley," George said. "They had that slogan, 'One More Pass.' Oregon State is like that. They have three guys, Blume, Radford, and Sitton, who play with amazing intensity. And then they can bring Conner off the bench. That's like having George C. Scott playing a minor role at the movies."

One of the highlights of the season came two nights later. At Washington, Marv Harshman had a good team, led by Bob Fronk, one of the guys in that Ainge-Blume-Radford-Stoutt high school class of 1977. With Marv's preparation and excellent players in Fronk and Andra Griffin, Washington was ready.

We were in trouble from the get-go. Washington got on top of us early and had a 44-34 halftime lead, shooting 59 percent and running its offense to perfection. Fronk had 15 points at the half. Johnson, meanwhile, had three fouls. His absence always hurt us not only in missing his points, but in allowing the opposition to overplay our outside shooters.

At the outset of the second half we went down by 12. There were 9,500 people in old Hec Edmundson Pavilion—many of them Oregon State fans—as the lure of seeing a top-ranked team, and the possibility of it losing, brought people out.

We scratched back into the game although we never did get Washington's offense under control. A Washington free throw on Johnson's fourth foul with a little less than a minute to play put Washington up, 83-79, but Conner drove for a basket to get us within two and we called timeout.

With half a minute left, we still found ourselves down by four, as Blume fouled Andra Griffin and he made both free throws. Our first defeat of the season seemed all but inescapable. With it would go the No. 1 ranking. That part would be a far greater disappointment for our team and our fans than it would be for me.

But we quickly cut it to two, as Conner flicked a pass to Holbrook, who scored from the lane. And then, with Washington trying to hold the ball, Ray Blume made a game-saving play. He caused one of the Washington guards to fumble the ball and then tied him up, creating a jump-ball situation with just 10 seconds remaining. He got the tip and we hurried it downcourt. Conner got a pretty good shot for the tie but missed and Johnson got the rebound. He shoveled it back in with a couple of seconds left and we had forced overtime.

With that mountain climbed, we won 97-91. We were almost beaten, but somehow we had survived. It was a titanic game, with Griffin and Fronk each scoring 25 for Washington, who shot 57 percent to our 59. Johnson tied his career high with 38 points, but that wasn't the most surprising aspect. A pretty mediocre foul shooter, Steve made 14 of 14 free throws—an Oregon State record still on the books.

We were in familiar form the next game, shooting .694 against UCLA at home and winning without much difficulty, 81-67. Johnson had 27 points on 12 of 17 and Blume had 18 on eight of 10.

The weekend ended with a strange win over USC, 55-48, as we ran our winning streak to 17 straight. We shot only .434. In the first half, we put on a big run to take a 16-point lead and it looked like it would be easy. But USC held us scoreless the final six minutes of the first half, scored 11 in a row and made it 26-21 at halftime. We could never get very comfortable, but we did prevail as Johnson had 25 points and 12 rebounds despite foul trouble that limited him to 28 minutes.

On to the Bay Area, where they had two sellouts to see the Orange Express, so dubbed by Darrell Aune, our play-by-play man.

At Cal, it was Blume night, as he hit 11 of 16 for 26 points and we won by 15. Stanford didn't try the slowdown tactic of the previous year, but the game was played at a measured pace with OSU leading 21-17 at halftime.

Johnson's frequent foul trouble became a factor again as he drew his fourth with 12 minutes left while we were leading by six. Fortunately, Radford stepped forward with 21 points (on nine of 13), and we got out alive, 62-57. It was yet another .600-plus shooting night, at .614.

A Mellower Miller?

We had an interesting weekend coming up. We were 19-0 and our No. 1 ranking was going to be severely tested. Because of our big season in 1980, we had finally wormed our way into a national television date against St. John's at the Nassau Coliseum on Long Island. Before that, we had to play Oregon in Eugene. It wasn't going to be an easy week. The itinerary called for us to play in Eugene Thursday night, bus to Portland, get a 7:00 a.m. flight to Kennedy Airport Friday, and then play Saturday afternoon.

Oregon had some talent and was ready for us, but our shooting simply wouldn't allow us to lose. We gunned in 15 of 20 in the first half, but were still ahead only 31-23. Then we went out and hit 14 of 20 in the second half—giving us a school-record .725 for the evening—and drew away, 78-61. Stoutt was eight of nine for 18 points, Johnson six of eight, Radford five of eight. That team could shoot.

It was on to New York the next day. We were about to play on Valentine's Day, and here we already had a 20-win season in the books. At that time, there was a raging debate going on about who should be No. 1: Virginia with Ralph Sampson, or us. *Sports Illustrated* ran a story on both of us, calling one team No. 1 and the other 1A. There were weeks when Virginia topped one poll and we won the other. One week, we tied. For eight consecutive weeks, we were either No. 1 or tied for it by either United Press International or Associated Press.

Unfortunately, we probably didn't do anything to endear ourselves to the nation when we went against St. John's. It was rather an ugly game. Lou Carnesecca, the colorful St. John's coach, said he used to have a nightmare in which his team never scored, and he said this one was like living that dream. We shot 46 percent in the first half, they shot 36. We led by eight.

We scored the first five points of the second half and St. John's never really threatened again. With Red Auerbach, the Celtic guru, a lot of professional scouts, the curious New York press, and the Big Apple basketball cognoscenti in attendance, we plodded to a 57-45 victory. We weren't impressive, but at least we won.

Some of my players during the latter half of my Oregon State tenure, including ones on that 1981 team, made the comment that they thought I had mellowed. I wasn't quite sure how to take that, although I suppose it's easier to coach a team that is coming closer to what you are trying to accomplish than one that is constantly struggling.

Perhaps it's true that I did mellow. I think in the early days, coaches could be more demanding. But society, the kids, everything else changed. I think I probably adjusted to the times, as much as anything else. I still maintained pretty good discipline, but it might not have been quite as harsh as when I was first starting out.

> **Dave Leach: "When I played, he was a lot more emotional and a lot tougher on players than when I was coaching with him. The garbage cans used to fly around a little in the locker room, and he was pretty good with some adjectives."**

Now we were 21-0, a school-record winning streak, and the question of when we would lose became a topic of conversation. At home, we had no trouble with Washington State. Next we had

Washington, the team that had come closest to us earlier. This time it was no contest. With the usual sellout crowd behind us, we took a ten-point halftime lead and won 89-63. It was another occasion when Steve Johnson had some remarkable numbers. Because of foul trouble, he played only 17 minutes, but he led us with 24 points. In the first six minutes of the second half, he had 15 points himself.

Then another testy weekend. We were going to play at UCLA Sunday afternoon and everybody was talking about that game, but on Friday night, we had USC and that proved to be a struggle. We were down 36-30 at halftime, and playing listlessly. We moved back in it early in the second half but USC hung tough. This was a pretty talented team, with Mo Williams, Dwight Anderson, and Jacque Hill.

I called two timeouts inside the nine-minute mark, but we couldn't pull away. It was 62-all after two free throws by Anderson. But Johnson took a pass from Blume for a layup with a little more than three minutes left, and then Johnson and Conner each hit two free throws. We managed a nine-point win, but that was deceiving.

Now we were 24-0, three games from an undefeated regular season, and we were looking at UCLA. As usual, this was a talented Bruin team, with Michael Sanders, Darren Daye, Cliff Pruitt, Rod Foster, and Michael Holton. It wasn't a big, intimidating group like it was in the old days, but quick and fast.

And the Bruins were at home. The UCLA mystique lived on well past the actual efficiency of its teams. Sometimes the opposition would take a look at those national-championship banners hanging in Pauley Pavilion, and it would be beaten before it began.

We played well early, taking a seven-point lead, but UCLA put together a 14-1 run, Sanders scoring eight of them. At halftime, we found ourselves shooting 59 percent but UCLA was at 60 even and ahead 45-39. We fell behind by eight, but soon, our size advantage with Johnson inside began telling. We caught up and went ahead by one, and it settled into a highly contested game. Conner hit two free throws to put us up four with less than eight minutes left. Then McShane, playing because Johnson had four fouls, hit Lester with a nice back-door pass and we led by six. Johnson fouled out, but McShane hit two free throws and took a back-door feed from Conner and we led by 11. UCLA closed and had the ball, down by four with 18 seconds left, but we limped on in.

It was fitting that Lester had the two clinching free throws with eight seconds left in an 82-76 victory. Lester was the man that day. He was simply marvelous, playing 40 minutes, scoring 17 points, and getting 10 assists and seven steals. He was everywhere.

We flew home happy, fulfilled and 25-0, conquerers of Pauley Pavilion for the first time in school history. We needed only to win two at home to finish the regular season unbeaten.

A Lousy Day

We nailed down a second straight Pac-10 championship against Arizona, but it was hardly a gimme. We led only by four at the half, edged it out to ten early in the second half, then stretched it into an 80-62 win. Johnson had another big night, with 22 points on eight of 11, Radford had 21, and we shot very well again, at .604.

It was obvious we weren't completely sharp, for several reasons. The UCLA win had been a tremendous high for all of us. For another, the talented Arizona State group was due in Saturday. And Saturday would be the last home game for our seniors and some parents would be on hand with all the attendant hoopla.

I've often wondered about how all the fanfare might have affected our performance that day. There was a full house, and it's a common practice to honor the seniors with a pre-game ceremony. We were pathetic that day. Perhaps our sentimentality was just the opening Arizona State needed. Perhaps we were less than sharp because the Pac-10 race had already been taken care of. Perhaps we simply weren't giving enough credit to Arizona State, which was a fearsome outfit when it got rolling.

At any rate, Steve Johnson had two fouls in a minute and a half, three with more than 11 minutes to go in the half. Arizona State got all the shots it wanted and went ahead 18-6 after 14 straight points.

It grew worse. Byron Scott was having a field day, with 17 points in the first half, and ASU led 40-17. The crowd was stunned. It was as if we had so thoroughly conditioned the people to winning that they couldn't believe their eyes. But Arizona State was fifth-ranked itself, so we weren't losing to a junior varsity team.

Down 40-20 at halftime, we couldn't make a run until Blume scored six straight points for us to get it back to 65-53 with about seven minutes left. ASU then scored the next six, and our unbeaten season was going to go down in flames. It was not a pretty sight.

> **Steve Johnson: "I think all the sentimental stuff got in the way, and Arizona State put on a slam-dunk clinic. I remember running home after the game to watch the highlights. I mean, they had a team: Byron Scott, Alton Lister, Fat Lever, Sam Williams, Johnny Nash. They had an NBA team. They had more talent than anybody."**

We were 26-1 instead of 27-0, and who is to say what sort of emotional hangover that left us? Losing a game at the end of the season is nothing novel, but when a team hasn't lost a game all season, when a team hasn't had the experience of picking itself back up, I suppose it's a consideration. But we had a mature group that should have been able to shed that disappointment.

The Kansas State Ending

Mention Kansas State to an Oregon State basketball fan, and he will immediately recognize the subject. It doesn't require any more explanation. The Kansas State game of 1981 will forever be one of my great disappointments. I had seen our 1970 Iowa team lose on a fluke play at the wire, and now another crushing loss awaited us.

There was an eerie similarity to the NCAA pairings of the year before. Just as most people had thought Weber State would beat Lamar on Weber's home court, there was little doubt that San Francisco, with seven-foot Wallace Bryant and guard Quintin Dailey, had a more talented team than Kansas State. But there are no easy roads in NCAA play. Our kids sat and watched as USF built a substantial lead and then Kansas State whittled it down and won. There might have been a feeling that we were fortunate to be drawing Kansas State, and if there was, it was wrong.

I still don't think we should have lost that game. Steve Johnson fouled out and the officials made two bad judgments on him in the second half. Without those, no question in my mind, we would have won.

We didn't play well, in any case. We did get out to a 26-19 halftime lead and seemed to have matters in hand. K-State scored the first four points of the second half, but we stayed in front, and Radford hit two perimeter jumpers to make it 39-28 inside the 14-minute mark.

Kansas State was a smart, disciplined team that didn't panic when it fell behind. With Ed Nealy and Rolando Blackman—still pro players, at last look—leading the way, K-State scored seven points and we suddenly had only a 42-39 lead midway through the second half.

We came back with the next two baskets, but Kansas State wouldn't be denied, answering with five points in a row to make it 46-44, OSU, at the five-minute mark. It was at that point that Johnson's successful hook in the lane was waved off and he drew his fourth foul.

With 3:44 left, Radford missed a one-and-one that would have put us up four. Twenty-one seconds later, Nealy tied it at 48 as Johnson fouled out.

At just over two minutes, K-State fouled Charlie Sitton and he went to the line for a one-and-one with the game tied. He too, missed. And now, Jack Hartman, the Kansas State coach, saw the opportunity to take the lead that his team had never once owned.

K-State ran the clock down expertly. I've been asked if I thought about a foul, to take our chances and at least give ourselves a final possession. No, because they kept the ball in the hands of their best foul shooters, including Blackman. The best defense we could throw at them seemed the way to go.

Ultimately, as every fan in orange and black knows, Blackman received the ball, dribbled and faded toward the right baseline. From 16 feet away, he cast off. I couldn't fault the defense; Mark was all over him.

Blackman connected perfectly. After we called a desperation timeout with two seconds left, Stoutt threw up a long attempt from half-court that didn't come close. Our season of glory had ended, 50-48.

It was a sour weekend in all regards. We were bothered by unsolicited phone calls in our hotel the night before the game. Pauley Pavilion, ostensibly a friendly site for a Pac-10 team, became a road arena when most of the fans took up with Kansas State, the seven-point underdog. Some of our contingent yelled back at them. Even as we were trying to hang on down the stretch, the brother of one of our players waved a sign disparaging UCLA.

We simply did not play very well. The final reckoning showed us having shot .476, an off-day for this team. We caused 20 turnovers, which should have been plenty on a day when Kansas State got only 33 shots. K-State was 16 of 18 from the foul line, we were eight of 12. In their last collegiate appearances, Johnson had 16, Blume 10, Radford 8, and Stoutt 4.

What that team accomplished was considerable, yet it lost a little bit of the glamour that day. It was a terrible loss. I think that team had a chance to get to the Final Four and do well.

Kansas State went on and won a third game in the tournament at Salt Lake City against Illinois, and played North Carolina for the West Regional title. Carolina won fairly handily and went on to lose in the national championship game to Indiana at Philadelphia on the day President Reagan was shot in an assassination attempt.

We buttoned up our season, and in the gloom of a joy ride ended, headed for home. There was a small, final consolation as we bussed north from Eugene on that somber Sunday. When we had left on Thursday, the little town of Monroe, population 400-plus, had turned out to wish us well. As we drove down Highway 99W, they came out of the schools and the stores, and the Long Branch Tavern, waving to commemorate our achievement. That one was scheduled. Now, as we returned, Monroe was there again, a couple of hundred people lining the streets in a hard rain, turning out for condolences.

We appreciated it.

15

From the Ashes, Another Title

One of the beauties of sport is that it always throws a curve. Just when we begin to assume someone is unbeatable, he is beaten. Indeed, a few hours before we lost to Kansas State, another No. 1 seed, DePaul, was upended by St. Joseph's. There are no certainties in sport. Its predictability is fragile. If it were not so, the gentlemen running the sports books of Las Vegas would not be turning such a large profit.

When we lost to Kansas State, there was a sense that the Orange Express had been terminally derailed. After all, we lost Johnson, who had shot an unheard-of .746 during our 26-2 season; and the 1977 recruiting class of Blume, Radford, and Stoutt. The popular view was that we were in need of a major rebuild.

Dreams and Dream Players

Strangely enough, Jimmy Anderson and I both thought before the 1981-1982 season started, that we could still win the Pac-10 title for a third straight year. I don't know why, call it a hunch. We had great faith in Lester; we had Charlie back; we had A.C. Green coming in. We couldn't see anybody in the Pac-10 who had a clearly better group than we did.

Those kind of seasons may just give a coach his deepest satisfaction. By the same token, we had been caught short late in the 1976 season when we lost Lonnie, and we finished with a bang. We were dealt a crippling blow in 1978 when Johnson went down with the broken foot, but we had hung tough and finished second in the conference without him. Now we were in that back-to-the-wall position: Nobody expected much. That's when I really got my kicks out of a season—when we would end up doing far more than anybody thought possible.

Perhaps more than even we thought possible.

We made a major score in the spring of 1981 with the signing of A.C. Green out of Portland. A.C. came out of Benson Tech, the school that produced Richard Washington and Rickey Lee. At the end of his sophomore year at Benson, A.C. was only about 6'3". By the time he began his junior year, he was 6'6" or 6'7", and his skills hadn't yet caught up with his body. He was a little on the clumsy side, not as agile as he had been. He wasn't the type of prospect who blooms early and remains in the eye of the recruiters. Oregon State, Washington State, and Utah were the only real suitors, and he eventually opted for us.

A.C. was just a joy to be around, a serious young man who had become a Christian before entering Oregon State. In airports, he would often be seen reading the Bible when other kids were off looking for video games. Before his senior year at Oregon State, he came to me and said, "I'm confused. I don't know whether I should become a pro basketball player or a minister."

I told him, "One of your chief goals in your church is to help people any way you can, right?"

"Yeah, absolutely," he said.

"Well," I said. "If you can make money as a pro, you can help many people. Your dad's a vet, drawing a pension, and his house isn't paid for, is it? Well, if you're a pro, you can pay it off, and that would certainly be of great help, wouldn't it? You can become a minister anytime."

Whether that bit of secular steering had anything to do with it, I don't know, but a few days later, A.C. came in and said, "I think you're right. I think I want to be a pro player first."

A.C. had great work habits. Particularly as the OSU days developed, he became more and more of a leader. Both he and Charlie just didn't know how to loaf on a basketball court. I remember one time at the Far West Classic, the coaching staff went to the tournament luncheon, and the traffic was so bad afterwards, we couldn't get to our practice at Memorial Coliseum on time. Well, 1:00 p.m. came and there wasn't a coach on the floor. So A.C. called the kids together and pretty soon, they were running the drills, full-tilt. That was the kind of person he was: We have an hour, we can't waste it.

Another important component of that team was a fellow who shouldn't even have been around. Danny Evans was a junior from Flint, Michigan, a fairly athletic 6' 5" wing type. He was quick, but his real strength was his shooting. After his freshman year, and then after his sophomore year, I advised him strongly to transfer. I didn't think he'd ever be a factor for us. I didn't feel there was any point in him wasting his time with us, and vice versa. His first two years, Danny never played enough to work up a sweat. Of course, he was matched against some pretty good talent on the team.

Finally, however, in the fall of 1981, Danny began to blossom. He had spent enough time in the system to begin to react to situations rather than have to ponder them. He became a starter for us. Later, however, I think Danny's stubbornness got the better of him. After the 1983 season, he was drafted by San Diego in the NBA, but he had been sick all summer with some sort of virus, and that was the year we were taking a pre-season trip to Argentina. We tried to convince him to stay amateur, go with us to Argentina — although his college eligibility was finished — hook on that year with Athletes in Action or somebody and produce a few more credentials.

We thought he was going to do that, but at the last minute, he just showed up in San Diego. He was cut and went over to Europe and played a year or two there.

Charlie was back that season as a sophomore, and the guard opposite Lester was William Brew, a strong, 6' 1" kid from Berkeley who couldn't shoot much, but played good defense.

There was no doubt about the straw that stirred this team. Lester led the club that year in points (14.9), rebounds (5.4), assists (5.1), and steals (3.0). I doubt that you'll see this happen very often anywhere. He simply lifted a bunch of ordinary people and made them champions. Actually, it wouldn't be fair to call A.C. and Charlie ordinary, but A.C. was coming in as a freshman, and Charlie was still young as a sophomore.

Steve Johnson has said that the 1981 team had egos, but put them aside to get the job done. Well, I think one of the beauties of the 1982 group was its absence of egos. First of all, there was no questioning who the real gifted, experienced player was; it was obviously Lester. And Lester's personality erased any potential problems in that regard. He was a fun-loving guy who had a great personality. He could melt the fans. He and I had a great relationship. Everybody loved him.

There was another player who had been in the news a lot but whose role, ironically, diminished as that season progressed. Greg Wiltjer was a seven-foot Canadian center whom we had known about when he was a high school player in British Columbia. We would need center help when Steve Johnson graduated after the 1981 season. Wiltjer would be that help once he had spent two years at North Idaho Junior College. We helped place him there.

Greg became a point of controversy when, after the 1980 season, his freshman year at North Idaho, he announced his intention to attend Washington. I think one of Marv Harshman's assistants showed up one night and hot-boxed the kid. I know for sure it wasn't Marv who went in and got him to commit. After Greg discussed the matter with his coach, Rollie Williams, he decided to stay at North Idaho for his second year, after which he opted for Oregon State. So early in the 1981-1982 season, it was Wiltjer who started for us at center. But as we moved into the Far West Classic, Greg sprained an ankle and it was slow healing. By the time he was ready to play, Danny Evans had supplanted him and ultimately, after that one season, Greg transferred up to the University of Victoria and has been playing on the Canadian Olympic team.

Coaching Honors and Bad Weather

We had been 52-6 over the previous two years and had had extensive national publicity. In 1981 and 1982, I received two national coach-of-the-year honors. I know there were Oregon State supporters who assumed that our newfound prominence would result in being able to recruit better, to entice a more highly acclaimed player into the program. Well, there are many dreamers in the world.

There were instances where we perhaps received a visit from a highly touted player because of the name we were building, but the basic format has never changed. We have had a limited number of great players from the state of Oregon over the years. Furthermore, just because we won, it didn't take away illusions relating to UCLA and other places. It was always hard, and always will be hard, to pull away a player from southern California if UCLA really wants him, or in some cases, even if another California school wants the player.

At the same time, the whole world started to recruit California. Up until this time, recruiting was certainly more regionalized. It was pretty much a given that a quality player in California would either attend one of the Pac-10 schools, or perhaps one of the lesser-conference West Coast schools. Suddenly Kentucky was recruiting in California; Syracuse was there; Villanova was there; Dean Smith was there for North Carolina. The boom in cable-TV early in the 1980s underscored that they were playing excellent basketball in the East, South, and Midwest.

At the same time we were having our glory years, Arizona and Arizona State were becoming entrenched as Pac-10 members. The Lever-Scott-Lister teams at Arizona State showed that if a recruit had had any aversion to attending those schools when they were not a member of the Pac-10, certainly that was removed now.

One thing that will never change in the Northwest is the weather. Probably in no other conference is there such a graphic difference in options for recruits in terms of the climate. I'll have to admit that when I came out from Iowa, one of the things I misjudged was the spring weather. I did know it rained, but I didn't understand how bad the springs could sometimes be.

Unfortunately, it seemed that, out of five or six weekends of recruiting, we might have one nice one in the spring. I did discover that if we were lucky enough to have a kid from Los Angeles in that particular weekend, we stood a chance with him. If somebody had just visited a California school the week before and everybody was running around in shorts, and then he came to my place and it was cold and rainy, I knew automatically we were wasting time and money. We weren't going to see that kid again.

We did assume the spring weather, at least, to be more moderate here when we left the snowfields of Iowa. Live and learn. As a basketball program, our lot in life was still primarily one of trying to uncover the player with untapped potential.

Our Third Pac-10 Title

We began that 1981-1982 season by thoroughly stifling a pretty good Bradley team at home, 81-55, and then going on the road before 22,000 people at Brigham Young and controlling that game, 55-44. We then lost to Portland on the road and came home the next night and handled Pepperdine, with A.C. making his first significant contribution of the season, with 17 points and ten rebounds off the bench. Little did we realize we would be seeing Pepperdine later in the season.

I suppose that our first real inkling that we had a pretty good basketball team came 8,000 miles from Corvallis, at the Suntory Ball in Tokyo. There, we beat up Pennsylvania and then won the title by defeating a Louisville team that had won the national championship two years before, 62-56. It was third-ranked at the time, and featured players like the McCray brothers, Scooter and Rodney, Derek Smith, Lancaster Gordon, and Jerry Eaves. We shot only 44 percent in that game—no more did we have the luxury of that 1981 team's .564 shooting—but we caused 21 turnovers. Rob Holbrook, a valuable sixth man on that team, helped considerably with ten points in 22 minutes.

We got our come-uppance, but good, in the Far West Classic. Idaho was also in the middle of a run of very good teams under Don Monson, and was still smarting from a bad, 100-59 beating we administered to a lesser Idaho club two years before.

In the semifinals of the Classic, Idaho got off to a 10-1 start, running the fast-break expertly as we did a poor job of rotating back. It was 32-20 at halftime and we were never really in it, losing 71-49. It was an educational game in that it showed we certainly weren't an overpowering bunch when we didn't come ready to play. At least we would have a chance later in the year to redeem ourselves against Idaho.

We were ready for the conference, however. In our opener at home against an Arizona State team much weakened by graduation, we rolled, 74-43. When our defense was playing hard, as it was then, we could be awfully good. We completed an opening sweep by beating Arizona, then went on the road and beat the Bay Area schools by a combined 74 points. After we thrashed Cal by 31, I had ready-made ammunition for the Stanford game.

Our history in the Bay Area had been to play well against Cal, start reading our press clippings, and then come out flat and struggle against Stanford. So I drummed on them about that, and our kids were anything but uninspired against Stanford. Conner was devastating against slower guards. We had it put away by halftime, and we ended up with an 81-38 win.

Now we were 11-2, 4-0 in league, and it seemed that the premonition Jimmy and I had about this team had a chance of materializing. We added three more wins to make it seven straight in the league, before stumbling, 74-68 at UCLA.

The next weekend we were home to the Bay Area schools, and I guess I added a little levity to what was already an enjoyable, crowd-pleasing team. In the latter stages of the first half against Stanford, I got up to say something, and as I sat down, the whole seam of my trousers split, from belt buckle to the back. At least I had a coat on. I managed to get the message to Jimmy, and we walked off the floor at halftime, kind of like two peas in a pod — as if we were huddling over some heavy strategy.

At halftime, while DeLoss Brubaker, our trainer, worked over my pants, running tape over the inside of them, I stood in my skivvies, socks, and coat and delivered my talk. I'm not sure it was received without at least a smirk or two. The emergency repair job worked all right, although I don't think I got out of my seat the entire second half. Finally when I got into my car to drive home, those pants gave out again.

That team continued on, overachieving all the way, and we won our third straight Pac-10 championship. I can't say it was the most enjoyable team I ever coached, but it was certainly right up there.

With the Pac-10 title already wrapped up, we lost 68-60 in the regular-season finale at Arizona State. In itself, the loss wasn't damaging, dropping our record to 23-4 and 16-2 in the league, but it did conjure worries among many people about whether it would carry over into the post-season. Taking note of our problems the previous two years in the playoffs, Rob Holbrook said if we didn't win, he was "going to find a hole somewhere and fall into it."

On the way back from our season-ending trip to Arizona, we got the word about the playoffs: We drew the winner of the Pepperdine-Pittsburgh game in a regional at Pullman.

A Better Team

There were reasons that Pepperdine, who defeated Pittsburgh, seemed to be an ominous matchup. It was rolling along with 12 wins in its last 13 games, and had some strong inside players. We had won by 15 in the earlier game in Corvallis, a motivating factor for them.

We edged out to a 33-27 halftime lead, making only four turnovers in 20 minutes. In the first ten minutes of the second half, Pepperdine sliced our eight-point lead to six on several different occasions, but each time we responded to push it back to eight. Three times it was Evans who answered Pepperdine baskets with a jump shot.

As the clock wound under ten minutes, we went to a delay game that we had installed just that week, with Sitton and Green doing much of the ball-handling out away from the basket. It frustrated Pepperdine. Jim Harrick, the coach, drew a technical foul inside the seven-minute mark, and we went up 55-41 after four straight free throws.

We eased in from there, never leading by less than 12. We were 70-51 winners, finally able to throw that play-off monkey off our backs. Evans had 18 points, Conner 16 and Sitton 14. Harrick was outspoken about disliking our slowdown tactics with the lead.

This was a team, ironically, that couldn't match the 1980 or 1981 groups for sheer talent. But it would be remembered for doing something those clubs never did.

Now we were matched up at Provo, Utah against Idaho, who, before our game, had played a cliff-hanger against Lute

Olson's Iowa team and won at the buzzer. The revenge factor was in our favor this time after Idaho's convincing win at the Far West Classic, and we pretty much controlled the game, winning 60-42. Conner was the man once more, with 24 points, ten rebounds and five assists, all game-leading figures. He hit ten of 14 from the floor, and we kept Idaho's good guards, Brian Kellerman and Kenny Owens, from going off too badly.

We led only 31-25 at the half, but Green and Conner hit the first two baskets of the second half and we had it our way after that. Still, the margin was a bit deceiving, as we led by ten with less than three minutes to go before Holbrook and Conner put it away with free throws. Again, the ingredients were defense and being able to control the ball when we needed.

Suddenly, with a team that had lost three players to the NBA the previous season, we were in the final eight of the NCAA tournament, just a game away from the Final Four at New Orleans.

Little did we realize what a giant step we were from that Final Four berth. So near, but yet so far. In retrospect, our regional was not really that tough. We hadn't had any trouble at all advancing to the regional final. Then we ran into the men.

We entered our game against Georgetown thinking they were not that good. Georgetown had beaten Wyoming in its opening game of the tournament and it was a close one. The game before we played them, they were extended to the last five minutes by Fresno State before finally blowing it open at the end. So we weren't scared.

Maybe we should have been. They hit us and hit us fast. Charlie took a charge on the baseline from a freshman named Patrick Ewing in the opening minute and we took hope. A few seconds later, Ewing picked up a loose ball at mid-court, and after a couple of huge steps, slam-dunked. We would never have the lead. I called timeout less than three minutes into the game—when we were behind only 4-2—and I never liked to do that. That was a little bit of an omen.

While Ewing controlled the middle, Sleepy Floyd began to hurt us everywhere. He scored 18 points in the first half and by the midway point of the half, we were behind by 15 points. It was 42-25 at halftime.

We were never in it. A.C. was a freshman and played like one, committing five turnovers. Charlie passed up some good shots with Ewing looming near the basket. The key shots Danny Evans made against Pepperdine weren't going down against this team. He finished four for 13 and the final score was 69-45.

Georgetown shot the lights out. We allowed a percentage of 74.4, which at the time was an NCAA tournament record. Oddly enough, Georgetown later surrendered what stands as the record today: Villanova shot 78 percent in the 1985 national championship game.

It was a miserable game for the coach and the players. There was nothing we could do. They took us apart. Had I been a spectator, I would have thoroughly enjoyed Georgetown's performance, it was so good.

Coming just a game from the Final Four, we felt our share of sorrow. Yet there was a sweet quality to it, too, knowing that we had simply been beaten by a better team and that our club had taken it just about as far as it had any right to.

After having lost three players to the NBA, we had finished 25-5, giving us a three-year record of 77-11 and 49-5 in conference play. I suppose you could say that was the end of our glory years at Oregon State. We would still produce some awfully good teams, but none that accomplished what the 1980-1982 clubs did. It was a wonderful run.

16

Winding Down

I would like to report that everything in the aftermath of the overachieving 1981-1982 team was sweetness and light. Unfortunately, it wasn't. By July of 1982, we were in the news again, and this time the stories weren't positive. We were being investigated by the NCAA. It's a sorry saga. It revolved around the selling of complimentary tickets by some of our players.

NCAA Infractions

To put it into perspective, 1982 was the first year that student athletes' complimentary tickets could not be sold. Until then, they could always be sold for face value. It had always been a means for the athlete to make a few dollars for spending money, and I still can't see anything wrong with it.

There was no denying my players had been selling tickets. What opened the thing up was a disgruntled student who left our program and decided to call the NCAA and tell them we were selling tickets. He, too, had been selling his tickets.

The events that triggered the investigation were these. Apparently, when we played at Brigham Young early in December of 1981, a contact was made by one or more of our players with a sporting-goods store owner in a shopping mall outside of Provo. When we finished our season at the West Regional there, these players exchanged sporting goods for their complimentary tickets, and some of them failed to leave the tickets for the gentleman. He became a ready source for the NCAA.

The player most implicated was William Brew, but he wasn't the only one. He may have helped some of the others get involved, but there were others. There was never really any bitterness between William and me. Eventually everything was straightened out. Of course, once you open the doors of the program to the NCAA, you're under investigation. When that happens, you get great news coverage, naturally. It becomes blown out of proportion.

We knew immediately that a few of our players had wrongly used their complimentary tickets, but there were other infractions reported by the NCAA that implicated members of the coaching staff. The major allegations were easily and quickly disposed of; we have always tried to operate within the confines of the rule book.

The coaching staff was guilty of committing several minor violations. Four of them involved auto transportation, twice from the Eugene airport to Corvallis, a distance of 35 miles, and twice within the city limits of Corvallis. We were also cited for more than the maximum three off-campus, in-person contacts with one prospective recruit.

There was heavier involvement by some boosters of the program, such as buying complimentary tickets from players. Other booster involvement included purchasing a commercial airline ticket for a player to travel to his home; furnishing a private plane for three players to travel from Corvallis to their homes; co-signing loans for two players; giving a microwave oven to a player; providing a loan so a player could purchase an automobile; and purchasing two pairs of shoes for a player.

It was always our policy to have our faculty athletic representative brief our team of current NCAA rules, and in 1981-1982, that included the new policy for complimentary tickets. The athlete is asked to read the material and then sign a statement that he understands it. That year, we also distributed fliers to fans attending our early-season games, explaining the new policy. So anybody, buyer or seller, who violated the rule did so deliberately.

We've always tried to investigate any rumor of wrongdoing by one of our players. So when a member of the NCAA infractions committee told me, "Coach, you should have been more aware of things," it raised my dander a bit.

I told them that I had had upstanding people in the community tell me to my face, "No, this is not true."

They say coaches should be aware of everything, but this just isn't realistic. You can try, but you're going to be surprised on occasion.

The NCAA investigation group takes a lot of heat for enforcing petty violations. Well, they're just administrators doing their job. When people rail on the NCAA, they're getting on people who are enforcing the rules that are legislated in by schools like Oregon State. The NCAA is us. We, and all the other schools, wrote those rules. I know some of the investigators personally. They don't believe they should be doing this, but it's on the books. So until we change those rules, let's not come down too hard on those policing them.

The whole incident reinforced my belief that sports merely mirrors society. I can't possibly see my way clear to say to a young man, "I don't want to see you talking to this guy or this woman."

You shouldn't control college students that much. They came to get an education. Sports merely emphasizes the good and bad of humankind. How can sports be perfect?

When the final reckoning was made in May of 1983, it did reveal a positive side to the whole mess. Said Frank J. Remington, chairman of the NCAA committee on infractions: "The investigations conducted by the NCAA and the institution did not indicate that any athletics department staff member was aware of or involved in the serious violations . . . It should also be emphasized that the university's assistance in developing information in this case was invaluable. In fact, the university uncovered approximately one-third of the serious violations found in the case and self-disclosed those violations to the NCAA. The university's disclosure of this information, which otherwise would have remained unknown to NCAA personnel, clearly demonstrated the institution's commitment to future compliance with NCAA legislation."

We were fined $342,000, the money we had made in the 1982 tournament. Three players lost eligibility for six games. We forfeited two future scholarships against the NCAA limit, but there were no television restrictions or post-season ban. I'd like to think the punishment fit the crime.

Twenty Wins and the NIT

We entered the 1982-1983 season essentially shorn of the key ingredients that had carried us in the glory years of 1980, 1981, and 1982. Lester was now off to the Golden State Warriors. My kids did me one early favor, winning the four-team tournament at Bradley, a place where I had never gotten out alive in 13 tries at Wichita. We struggled mightily early in the conference season, starting off 1-4 before reeling off seven consecutive victories.

We suffered too many lumps to be considered for the NCAA tournament for a fourth straight year, but we settled for the NIT and did quite well. We beat Idaho and New Orleans handily at our place, the latter win bumping us to 20 victories for the fourth straight year. Then Boyd Grant's Fresno State team came to town, played the usual great defensive game, and ended our season, 76-67, on the way to the NIT championship. It was the second victory of the year for Fresno at our place.

My First Contract

We were back in the trophy room the next season, sharing the Pac-10 championship with Washington. We were swept on the road early by the Washington schools to put us in a hole, but strung together ten league wins in a row.

Interspersed was a one-point loss at Michigan State in one of the rare national network TV appearances by Oregon State. We made a grand total of two of those in my years there, even with some pretty fair teams. Despite going 77-11 for three years, we were still an unknown commodity nationally to many people. I think that pretty well illustrates the imbalance involved in television appearances.

Near the end of the season, Don Monson brought his first Oregon team to face us at Gill, and tried the old slowdown tactic. It was quite effective, but his center, Blair Rasmussen, had an 0-for-7 shooting night and we survived, 29-23. That ploy bothered many people, but not me.

We were paired that year opposite West Virginia in a regional at Birmingham. It was the first time we had played in a full 64-team field without having a bye in the first round.

It was a sluggish performance. We had a tenuous lead through most of it, but couldn't pull away. Finally, with the game tied, we were holding the ball for a final shot inside the 10-second mark when we made a lazy pass out front. A guard named J.J. Crawl intercepted, blew in for a layup, and that was it. We didn't score in the final five and a half minutes. We lost 64-62, capping a 22-7 season.

I think it was about this time I did something historic. I signed a contract. Dee Andros, my athletic director, came in one day and said he thought he'd feel better if I had a contract. That was my only contract—it was for three years, after I'd been at Oregon State for 15 years. It didn't mean a thing. The arrangement had always been that unless I did something terribly wrong, they'd have to notify me two years in advance. That was good enough.

I felt that I wanted my own freedom. If I wanted to leave, I could leave, and I didn't have to have three or four years on my contract. So through the Wichita and Iowa days, I did not have a contract. I did have tenure at Wichita and Iowa, and I thought I would have tenure at Oregon State, but the year I came, the new president decided coaches would not have tenure. Personally, I always felt there should be freedom at both ends, both for the university and for the coach.

I didn't even tell Jean when I signed it. I didn't realize any announcement would be made. She heard it over the radio a couple of months later. Needless to say, I heard about that.

Another NCAA Tournament

A.C. Green was our senior leader in 1984-1985, averaging 19 points and 9.2 rebounds. We got off to a phenomenal start at 15-1, but we were probably playing over our heads. We won the Classic without too much difficulty, beat UCLA at home, and then upset Washington on the road in a game in which we played five kids for 40 minutes apiece.

We were spotty after that 15-1 start. We lost a double-overtime game at home to Arizona State, and later, a two-pointer to USC when a fellow named Larry Friend cast up a shot from his hip from 18 feet with one second left.

There would be some heavy irony in that. In the last game of the season at USC, Oregon State needed to win to stay alive for the NCAA tournament. Friend missed two free throws down the stretch that would have won it for USC. We won in overtime, 60-58 — the same score by which we lost to USC earlier.

We did make the NCAA, but didn't get any particular favor from the selection committee. We were sent to Notre Dame to play the Irish on their home court. Actually, we acquitted ourselves well. We fell behind by 13 points early in the second half, but came all the way back to tie it. Then we let it get away again down the stretch and lost, 79-70.

We certainly have had our share of problems in NCAA play, and it's one thing I've never been able to understand. It doesn't seem fair, it doesn't seem right, but you can't change history. I came to believe that it really hurt us having a bye in the 1980 and 1981 playoffs, as strange as that seems. At that time, there was upset after upset of teams with first-round byes. I was glad to see the tournament expand to 64 teams to do away with those.

At Ogden in 1980, I remember talking to Ladell Anderson, a rules committeeman, about the situation. We couldn't even go into town until after the first-round games were over and somebody lost. There was no motel space. They had to send somebody home first. Then the first time we could practice there was, I think, about 8:30 the night before. Lamar had been there, had a good game and won.

In 1981 at Los Angeles, we had an unfortunate incident where the phones rang much of the night in our kids' rooms. The clerk at the front desk was a foreign student who didn't understand the directive to shut off calls to the players.

One player got a call from a man claiming to be a lawyer, threatening a lawsuit on behalf of a woman whom the player did not know. We got the phones shut off at around midnight. Then a call came to my room, the purported lawyer giving me the same story about the player. Finally, Mike Slive, an attorney with the Pac-10 office, handled the next call and said he had made arrangements with the federal courts for an appointment with the caller the next morning regarding the woman's complaint, and that ended it. I don't think that contributed anything to the loss, but again, Kansas State got its victory before we were there.

We've lost just about every way imaginable, on last-second shots, on steals at the end, their shots falling and ours not. It even seemed to carry over to Jimmy's first team last year, losing the way they lost against Ball State.

> **Steve Johnson: "I've thought about this a lot. The only flaw I could see in Ralph's system was that it didn't allow for someone to step outside their, quote, unquote, role to take control of the game. It was dependent on all the ingredients clicking, and if they weren't, or if one wasn't, it was like a domino effect.**
>
> **"In the NCAA, you play within the system, but you really have to give guys their freedom to go out and play. I remember the Kansas State game, it was really frustrating for me in that they were collapsing from the outside. I wanted to catch the ball a little farther out and make something happen."**

My Third and Last Losing Season

The year 1985-1986 was probably the most disheartening season of all my coaching years. It turned out to be the third and last losing season I ever had. There were good reasons for the other two. The first was my initial year at Wichita. The second was that star-crossed first year at Oregon State. It's hard to explain this one, other than that team did not develop a real leader. We had four seniors on the team, which should have produced one or two good leaders, but it did not happen. The last half of the season that team was like a rowboat without a rudder.

We got off to a 9-3 start and somehow finished 12-15. What seemed to start our downfall was a game at Arizona. We were off to a 4-1 conference start and playing at a very hostile site. Darrin Houston hit a shot from outside to give us a one-point lead with three seconds left, but Arizona took timeout, threw the ball from our baseline all the way down to the opposite free-throw line, where it came loose. Craig McMillan picked it up and drove in for a layup that beat us. We went on to play much more poorly and lose at Arizona State. It was all downhill from there. That season broke our skein of consecutive post-season appearances at seven.

At least one good thing came out of that season. The day after we lost that crushing game at Arizona, we learned that our center, Jose Ortiz, had gained an additional year of eligibility. We had known about Jose as a high school player in Puerto Rico, but his club owner wasn't about to let him come to the States. Finally, the owner consented and called us, but the NCAA had to rule on a second year of eligibility because of Jose's club participation in his home country, and it was granted. Good thing. Jose was one of the few positive things we had going on that 1985-1986 team, leading us in scoring and rebounding.

Help on the Way

More help was coming. We managed to recruit a sassy, gifted point guard from Oakland named Gary Payton. The minute you saw him play, you said, "Hot dog (no pun intended), here's a player."

His hand-eye coordination and peripheral vision were second to none. With a flick of the fingers, he could pass a ball 50 feet on a straight line. He saw everybody. St. John's had a shot at him and passed, so we got him. Some people didn't appreciate his court demeanor, but I did. I couldn't have had anybody any better, or easier, to coach. He was so intense. When he'd talk to me— "What do you want to do next, Coach?"—he was shaking, he was so intense. People would say, "He's jawing at Coach Miller."

He never jawed at Coach Miller once.

He was blessed not only with hand-eye coordination, but good ears. In timeouts, he never missed a thing that was said. When he was a freshman, I told him, "Prove to me you're one of the five best defensive players, and you'll start."

He started from the very outset. He was named the Pac-10's defensive player of the year as a freshman. His first year, I told him, "Your ambition is to be a pro, right? Well, then you've got to learn to shoot from the outside. Guards your size are a dime a dozen if you can't learn to shoot from outside. Anybody with your coordination can learn to shoot from anywhere."

Well, Gary worked a lot with Freddie Boyd on his shooting and really improved it. Gary never fought you. If I said, "Gary, you're talking too much, let your ability speak for you," he'd say,

"OK, thanks."

Very few people know the Gary Payton I knew. I don't think of him as cocky at all. He has supreme confidence in his ability, but there's that fine line between supreme confidence and cockiness. I appreciate those qualities, that persona that says, "I've been through it, give me the ball."

I like that in a player.

Gary finished the 1989-1990 season as the NCAA's second leading career assist man to Sherman Douglas. If he had had people to help him, he may have set a record that might have lasted many years. He's never had a great postman except for Ortiz, and that was for a single season. He's never had other players with comparable ability to catch the ball and see people. So many times, his great passes resulted in players getting fouled going to the basket or in missed layups. I don't think there's a better passer alive than Gary. He's the best there is.

Gary began his career in fitting fashion. He popped a three-point shot the first time he touched the ball in our 1986-1987 opener at Texas-El Paso, we built a big lead and won. Later that year, we fell behind by 22 points in the first half at UCLA but made a memorable comeback from a 32-10 deficit to take it into overtime. Payton's bank shot gave us a three-point lead at one stage, but Reggie Miller's shot broke a tie and defeated us at the buzzer. Payton showed the Pauley fans something, with 18 points and 12 assists.

We had another cliffhanger—that's not even a strong enough description—against Oregon. In Eugene, the Ducks, playing marvelously, had us down by eight points with 40 seconds left, 63-55. But Eric Knox hit a three-pointer from the wing, and after a missed free throw by Oregon, Knox banked one in for another three points. We were within two. We created a traveling violation with 11 seconds left, took a timeout and got the ball to Bill Sherwood in the corner. Bam. He hit with two seconds left and we won, 64-63. This was the first year of the three-point shot, and if we didn't grasp the impact of it before then, this game surely brought it home.

After that, we hit a horrendous tailspin, losing six straight after getting out to an 18-4 record. Our fate was the NIT. We managed to win at Albuquerque against New Mexico—no mean feat—on another athletic, three-point shot by Knox with two seconds left, but we finished a 19-11 year by falling to California at home.

My Short, Quick Team

As my years at Oregon State wound down, I guess I acquired something of a reputation as a ball-control coach. I was perceived by many people as somebody who was trying to keep the game within my control by reining in the players and dictating that we weren't going to run extensively.

After A.C. Green went to the Lakers and succeeded there, suggestions were made that nobody had known whether he could fit in with them because we didn't run at Oregon State. Well, there was plenty of opportunity to see how fast A.C. was. Anybody who knew basketball knew he could run and catch the ball.

One of my coaching tenets is that personnel dictates what your strengths are. The fast-break has always been part of my philosophy, going way back to 1935, when Chanute was the only team in the Kansas state tournament that used it. When I became a college coach, I was probably more of an offensive coach than I was a defensive one, but then I came to the conclusion that offense was not the thing that wins games.

The ability to fast-break depends on your personnel. In the Steve Johnson period, we used the fast-break all the time. If you have guards, and can get the ball back, you can run. True, in some of the later years, we weren't running nearly as much, but we didn't have the guards we needed to run in those days. Until we got Gary Payton, we frequently didn't have that type of guard, nor did we have the rebounders.

Perhaps the best example of this is the 1978 team that had Steve Johnson for a few games, but then lost him. With him, we could do some running. Without him, we had no rebounding, and we had freshman guards. So we played it closer to the vest. Circumstances dictate strategy.

It was hard not to like our 1988 team. We started nobody taller than 6' 6". The lineup was Payton, at 6' 3"; Knox, 6' 2"; Bill

Sherwood, 6' 6"; Will Brantley, at 6' 4"; and Earl Martin, 6' 5".

As we did in my final years at OSU, we used quickness and speed to create a big imbalance in turnovers. We weren't going to out-rebound teams or bother teams with much inside scoring, but we could do a lot of damage with our defense. It was a rewarding season. We won the Classic once more but then stumbled off to a 3-4 conference start after losing two in Washington. We clicked off nine wins in ten tries in the Pac-10 at that point, including an important win at Stanford.

In the Pac-10 tournament, probably needing to reach the finals to gain an NCAA berth, we did just that. We beat Washington badly and survived a sluggish game in double overtime against Washington State, as Payton led off each overtime with a three-point basket.

Bill Sherwood was hobbling on a bad ankle. We sat him out of our Arizona loss, and in the NCAA, partly because of Sherwood's condition, we simply couldn't contend with Louisville's inside strength. In a first-round game, we scrapped to a tie at halftime but got worn down with size in the second half and lost 70-61.

It was about then that we decided I would coach one more season. I would be 70 in March of 1989, and that would be the logical time to call it quits.

> **Jean Miller: "I definitely wanted him to retire after the 1988 season. We had won the Classic, he had been honored by the NIT as its Man of the Year. I felt that going through another year would be anti-climactic. I was looking forward to a more relaxed lifestyle, and I assumed Ralph felt the same.**
>
> **"It wasn't until the season was almost over, and we were discussing it with our children, that it became apparent I was in the minority. That was when I first realized, Ralph was not thinking that way at all. Ralph truly wanted to coach one more year and they felt he should be given the opportunity."**

One More Year

It was after the 1987 season that Oregon State made the announcement Jimmy would succeed me as head basketball coach. Other schools had begun to use my possible retirement as a negative in recruiting, and we needed to clear the air and state that the system that OSU had been playing for so long would continue under Jimmy.

Actually, the last time I had promised a recruit that I would stay for his four years, was Charlie Sitton back in 1980. Whenever it came up after that, I made no guarantees. The 1987 announcement was open-ended. All it said was that Jimmy would succeed me. It didn't say when.

> **Jim Anderson: "A lot of people tried to say I was sitting here all these years, coveting his position, but it wasn't that way at all. Ralph, for being a boss, was one of the most trusting people you can imagine. I can't trust people under me like he did. He could go a week, two weeks and not even ask a question. We'd have to go in to him, and ask what's going on.**
>
> **"No, I wasn't getting itchy about when he'd retire. After you've been coaching for 28 years, then it comes 29 and 30, what's another year? Ralph was giving me a lot of responsibilities. It wasn't like he was short-cutting me.**
>
> **"I felt very strongly I'd get the job. He supported me, the old school supported me. There was no reason to think it wouldn't come about.**
>
> **"Lanny was very good about it. I think he understood the whole gamut. After he was here for a period of time, he could see the handwriting on the wall, and he never, ever tried to be political or get into lobbying."**

Gary Payton helped get my final season off to a good start. We beat Portland, 106-59, and he had a so-called triple-double, with

20 points, 14 rebounds and 11 assists. Once again, we won the Far West Classic, the eighth time in my tenure we accomplished that.

Gary had 41 points, then a career high, and we beat Washington State at home. We were hanging in the title race until a third conference loss, at UCLA. But we finished quite respectably, going 13-5 for third place. In the home finale, many of the support people on the floor wore tuxedos. Nice of 'em.

From the standpoint of a send-off, it was a wonderful year. Led by Gary's 20.1 points a game, the team competed well, finishing 22-8 and giving me an 11th season in my career with 20 wins or better. The final tally was 674 wins and 370 losses. That's a lot of pre-game naps, a lot of inveighing against officials' calls. And a hell of a lot of satisfaction.

Then there was the hoopla off the court. At every site, I was treated to a royal reception with gifts and mementoes. People couldn't have been more wonderful.

Well, I guess Evansville could have.

17

For the Good of the Game

$\mathbf{B}$ack in 1954, when I was at Wichita, I spoke in front of a service-club gathering and was asked if I had any suggestions for the rules committee.

"I'd like to see them put that basket up to 12 feet," I was quoted then, 35 years before my retirement. "There should be no such thing as a cheap goal in basketball."

Three Key Rules

It wouldn't be the last time I offered an opinion for the consumption of the rules committee. Some consider that one a revolutionary idea, but it isn't, especially in the perspective of evolution of the rules since the 1930s.

The center jump was eliminated my senior year in high school. At that time, there were three major rule changes, and they established the format for the game of today. First, they eliminated the center jump, which had mandated a jump ball after each made basket. Second, they created the three-second lane violation. And third, they created the 10-second backcourt violation.

Just as two of these rules did, the great majority of rules since the 1930s have been implemented to reduce the effectiveness of the big man. Even before the days prior to the inclusion of basketball into the Olympics, the Japanese wanted to form two divisions for basketball, one for people over six feet and one for those under. The Japanese, of course, had very few big guys and the U.S. had many of them.

The controversial rule was the elimination of the center jump. It made the game one of continuous court action, and there was hardly unanimity for it. As I've said, Dr. Allen opposed it and Dr. Naismith violently opposed it. They feared great heart and lung damage if the game were allowed to be speeded up.

I can remember playing with the center jump. In 1935, when we won the state title in Kansas, there was one particular game when we were behind by six or seven points with two minutes to go. We scored and then controlled all the following tips so that in the last two or three minutes of the game, our opponents never had a ball possession. It seems unthinkable today, but that's the way it could work.

I also remember seeing when I was in junior high, an AAU game played without the three-second count. The center for this team simply parked in the lane and all he did was wiggle from side to side. The new rule, of course, started a trend for movement. Back in my dad's day, they played a different scheme, in which they had a standing guard and a four-man offense. The standing guard would, as the name implies, simply stand to protect the basket. So they have made some progress since then.

The 10-second count provided that the poor defense didn't have to cover the whole court. Prior to the 10-second count, you could take the ball into forecourt, go into backcourt and do that all night long. They figured that was a little unfair. So in implementing that rule, they opened the door for full-court pressure defenses. In the perspective of the old rule, what the 10-second count did was help to herd the offense into forecourt, and thus decrease the amount of space the offense could use to control the ball.

Those three rules were really the ones that established the format for our game today. All the rest of these rules, even the shot clock and three-point shot, did not touch the basic format we've used in basketball since 1936-1937. They called that the Golden Era of the game and it rightly deserves that title. Even the jump shot, the byproduct of Hank Luisetti's one-hander, was in evidence in the late 1930s. The decade of the 1930s really made modern-day basketball, and no decade will ever challenge for the accolade.

The only thing different about the sport today is television. And it's been messing up the game ever since it came in.

Big Men

Dominating big men also created some changes in the 1950s. Bill Russell and Wilt Chamberlain scared the pants off basketball coaches. They forced many changes all by themselves.

Bill could commit basket interference and you sometimes didn't even know it. In those days, a player could put both hands over the rim in following a shot in, and he did, frequently. Referees couldn't tell whether the outside shot was good, or whether he had pushed it in. The rulemakers changed that.

More spectacular was the way Chamberlain used to shoot free throws. Of course, Wilt was a terrible free throw shooter at Kansas so Dr. Allen concocted a new free-throw style for him. Upon receiving the ball from the official, Wilt would go back beyond the free-throw circle, start to run, take off at the free throw line and dunk his free throws. As a result of that, we have a plane at the foul line and only the arms and hands can be over it during the shot.

Then there was a novel out-of-bounds play on the baseline for Wilt. Kansas would take the ball out directly underneath the basket and simply throw it over the backboard, and Wilt would catch it and slam-dunk. Pretty effective. So that went out at the same time. Yet, those revisions during the 1950s were only small changes affecting specific shots. The new rules of the 1930s revolutionized the game.

Foul for Profit

One of my pet peeves with today's rules is what I call the foul-for-profit—fouling at the end of the game when behind in hopes that your opponent will miss free throws. They've got to do something here in a hurry. I see they've instituted a rule that provides for two shots after the tenth foul of a half, and that should help, but it doesn't go far enough. The last four or five minutes in college basketball have become a most boring activity. It's a parade to the free throw line.

Foul-for-profit has created problems for the rules committee, relating to the spirit of the rules, and specifically to the interpretation of intentional fouls. Since 1891, a personal foul was intended to penalize the offender and his team. Ideally, everyone would operate within the spirit of the rule, but there will always be some people who believe that rules are made to be broken or bent.

Traditionally, an intentional foul carried the most severe penalty—ejection from the game. Then a new interpretation was made, allowing any attempt to get the ball to be classified as unintentional. That speeded up the era of foul-for-profit. Deliberate fouls are premeditated and usually ordered from the bench, as any lip reader can attest. I would like to see the offended team have a choice in the matter of shooting or not shooting the one-and-one in the latter stages of a game.

It has been suggested that this could pave the way for a farcical situation in which an offensive team simply will not shoot the free throws. Potentially, you could have a situation where the offense takes the ball out of bounds 25 times in one minute, declining the opportunity to shoot the free throw, and the only risk to the defense would be losing players because of foul trouble.

If it becomes clear that this is the offense's intention, the defense might then begin a roughneck style, figuring that it has nothing to lose. Well, if we're going to screw it up, let's screw it up good.

I recall back in 1983, we had a graphic example of how the foul-for-profit ploy can work. We were playing Arizona State in Bob Weinhauer's first year there. Weinhauer had Byron Scott, the outstanding guard. He was a friend of William Brew, our guard, and with about 12 minutes left, he said to William, "Better get rid of the ball as quickly as you can every time you get it, because if you don't, I'm going to foul you."

At that time, we had about a 25-point lead, but from then on, Arizona State fouled us on virtually every possession. It worked. They would come down and score with Scott and Paul Williams while on too many occasions, we would miss or hit only one free throw. ASU cut the deficit under ten, but we finally ended up winning 108-93, in a Monday-night TV game that took two hours, 20 minutes. We established a Gill Coliseum record for free throws attempted with 63, hitting 46.

It's ironic that our gym was also the site that year of the beginning of the run that brought foul-for-profit to national attention. North Carolina State's march to the national championship began in Corvallis, when it benefited from missed free throws by Pepperdine and Nevada-Las Vegas, and won narrowly both times. North Carolina State would go on to make use of foul-for-profit again in the tournament, including the championship game against Houston. As a result, the tactic has become commonplace.

The Basket

I have always advocated raising the basket to 12 feet for college and professional use. The 10-foot basket should remain in place for the high school and lower levels of competition. While most of the rules in the past 55 years have dealt with limiting the domination of the big man, the rules committee has overlooked the most fundamental way to solve that problem—raising the baskets to 12 feet.

Remember, the basket is ten feet high only because of happenstance. Only the fact the railing on the running track at Springfield College was ten feet above the gym floor dictated where Dr. Naismith nailed the peach basket, and at that time, a height of 5' 6" was considered pretty tall.

I realize that the cold logic in that is not necessarily the yardstick we should use in determining how high the basket goes. To many people, the appeal of the game centers around the acrobatics of people like Michael Jordan and Dominique Wilkins. To raise the basket would be to remove the intimacy their ability allows them with the hoop, but I'm not one of those who thinks the game revolves around the dunk shot.

Most people seem to agree that the concept of bringing the smaller man back into the game would enhance the sport. Through the years of rule changes designed to curb big men, however, they continue to be a dominating factor. Almost all big men have limitations. These are exposed when they cannot simply camp under the basket. The speed, quickness, agility, and ball sense of big men cannot be compared to the likes of Michael Jordan, Isiah Thomas, and many others.

Consider the effect on the big man of a 12-foot basket versus a 10-foot one. The 12-foot basket would not allow a big man to control the boards simply by camping underneath, because the ball will carom off the hoop or backboard much higher and farther than from a 10-foot hoop. As a result, the offensive end of the floor would have to be widely spread for rebounding—and quickness, judgment, and speed would dominate the boards.

Shooting? Adapting to 12-foot baskets will be no problem for outside shooters. Give them time to practice on the raised basket and percentages will not drop to any significant extent. As a matter of fact, for 20 years our players used to improve shooting techniques by practicing occasionally on a 12-foot basket. Probably the biggest adjustment would be in shooting the layup, because the dunk shot would now be passe.

My former assistant, Brice Durbin, conducted a test years ago in the state of Kansas. As director of the Kansas High School Activities Association, he oversaw an experiment in which 40 teams played 20 games with a raised basket of 11 feet, three inches. He gave all the teams one week of practice. In only one game did the shooting percentages on 11-3 baskets drop below that averaged with 10-foot baskets. That's a pretty strong recommendation for higher baskets.

I've always said, raise the basket to 12 feet and show me somebody who can dunk on it, and I will applaud. Under today's circumstances, it's merely another form of layup. I still call it the idiot's delight.

Raising the basket would certainly trim out the phases of the game that raise the blood pressure of the spectators, but I think it would improve the game. It would be nice if fans could begin to fully appreciate the art of basketball. However, in my opinion, the baskets won't be raised until somebody breaks his neck. And it may happen.

The Shot-Clock and Three-Point Line

As we head further into the 1990s, the one thing I can see for sure is the shot-clock requirement going down, from 45 seconds to 35 and 30, and probably eventually, to 25. I know I'm in the minority, but no one has done anything to convince me that the clock or three-point line has ever been needed.

The average shot was going up about every 20 seconds

anyway, so why did we need a clock? Why? Because television didn't like the few games where somebody wanted to use ball-control. Well, ball-control should always be a part of the game because it gives the underdog a better chance to win.

The shot clock has ended the extreme stall, but I am convinced that the clock and the three-point shot have increased the use of zone defenses. Zones saw greater usage during the 1985-1986 season when only the clock had been instituted by the rules committee. To counteract the increase in zones, the three-point shot was also voted in, resulting in a rise in scoring but no decrease in zones. Coaches reason that zones force more outside shots and because the shot must be taken within 45 seconds, and the zone slows the pace of an offense, zone defenses are here to stay.

The three-point line at 19'9" is simply too close to the basket. You have trouble getting people to believe this, but even when I played in the mid-1930s, there were players you had to pick up at mid-court. If you didn't, they'd stop and let that old two-hand bomb go. And they could hit it.

One of the things I'll always remember was playing USC in the Western regionals in 1940 when I was a junior at Kansas, the year we lost to Indiana for the national title. We made a basket with about eight seconds to go, and it proved to be the game-winner in a 43-42 contest. USC called a timeout to set up its last shot. It didn't resemble the kind of play you'd see today.

A fellow named Morrison took the ball. It was my unfortunate task to be his defensive assignment. Morrison was dribbling, and suddenly, about ten to 15 feet from the half-court line, two big people form a wedge right at me. I'm looking at these two big guys and I couldn't get around. So Morrison stops about 55 feet away, shoots that ball and all I could say was "Oh, no."

That shot was dead center, but it was about 1/32nd of an inch too long.

There were people that were always able to shoot that long shot. My father could do it. Even at 40, he was standing out there, flipping them in. These long shooters of today couldn't even hold their own with some of those shooters in the two-hand days.

The three-point line should be extended to 21 feet. A few years ago, we took a Pac-10 all-star team to Norway and Sweden, and we couldn't believe the warm-ups. Nobody took a shot inside of 20 feet. We had no trouble defending the guards or wings, but we had trouble with the postmen. They could shoot 20-footers. Our players did not believe they would try them. They were wrong.

Everyone agrees the 1990 NCAA tournament was one of the most exciting ever, and it will be contended that the three-point shot had much to do with that. I disagree. Parity is the reason. Sixty-four teams were in there and they can all play good basketball. Who came closest to Nevada-Las Vegas? Ball State. Where's Ball State? I know that league, the Mid-American Conference, has always been tough in basketball, but few Oregonians were aware of it.

I think something should be special to merit extra points. A 20-foot shot—no way. I'd rather see three for somebody who made a layup off half-court offense, a back-door cut. That's what basketball is all about. With the three-pointer, the quick shot clock—I believe it is inevitably going to be shortened—then we will be playing the pro game. I don't think that's necessarily what we should be seeking.

The Hook Shot

I see other changes in the game that bother me. The hook shot has gradually been disappearing from the college and high school scenes. It has returned to a degree to the pro game, but it is increasingly scarce among colleges and high schools.

I think a post player without a hook shot is like a rowboat without oars. Steve Johnson was the last player we recruited at Oregon State who knew how to use the hook shot when he arrived, and he still holds the NCAA season field-goal accuracy record at .746.

The hook is an excellent tool for learning how to pivot. Shots are taken closer to the hoop. It's a difficult shot to block, and the postman can see cutters more clearly. Pete Newell, whose California team won the 1959 national championship, runs a big men's camp during the summer, and he has long lamented that traditional post skills like the hook have gone by the wayside.

I used to encourage our players to use the hook by asking them this: "Who's the best postman in basketball?"

"Jabbar," they'd answer.

And I'd say, "Well, what does he shoot most of the time? The sky-hook. If the hook shot's good enough for Jabbar, don't you think it might be good enough for you?"

Just as the old-fashioned hook has basically disappeared, screening the boards has become a lost art. Way back in the 1960s, both John Wooden of UCLA and Ed Jucker, who coached the national championship teams from Cincinnati, had clinics in which they said, "We no longer screen out on the boards. We just go get the ball."

Well, if you had Jabbar, that was not difficult. And Jucker had three great rebounders in Paul Hogue, George Wilson, and Ron Bonham. Wooden's and Jucker's influence became apparent for some time after that; few high school coaches were teaching how to screen the boards.

Run-Shoot-Run

Many coaches are follow-the-leader types. Now the Loyola Marymount style may catch on with some coaches. I'm sure there will be some that try it. It'll be fine if they've got the shooters, but in many ways, it's not sound if you don't play defense. Paul Westhead, the former Loyola coach, concentrated much more last year on defense than they ever had before.

They've certainly made a lot of noise and been popular for television. But the test of the Loyola system will be coming. Paul was fortunate in that he had some hellish players. Now many of those fine shooters he had are no longer there and we'll have a chance to see how well it's going to work with more average personnel. Loyola is a good example of an old belief I hold, which is nothing has changed for years in basketball, and what are taken to be innovations today are merely reorganizations of old concepts.

Maury John, the coach at Drake University when I was at Iowa, played that way when he came from junior college. You've seen it throughout the history of basketball. It used to be called run-shoot-run. The pros played it when they became prominent in the 1950s.

Paul Westhead, I think, is primarily an offensive-minded coach, but I think he recognized in 1989 what defense could do for his system because his 1990 team improved greatly in that area. His team was certainly enjoyable to watch.

My Practice Program

I'd like to include a few words on the simplicity of the practice program that served me well through the years. Among those who would aspire to be a coach, the question has been heard many times over the years: How do you become a successful coach? Let's start with a few personal concepts. Coaches are merely teachers, teaching physical skills and related concepts for competitive purposes. The mark of a good teacher is the ability to simplify the subject matter for easy consumption.

In basketball, the basic requirements have not changed much over the past 50 years. Drills are the primary teaching aids for education. It is important to remember that there is no time for thought during a game. Players must rely on automatic responses. Reactions should be conditioned in the drill program. Some coaches get carried away with drills, doing a thousand different things. Here is our program, which includes only six drills:

The first drill is what I call the normal setup (layup) drill, using two lines. The passer receives the ball, stops at the free throw line area, pivots and makes the pass to the shooter, then rebounds the shot. The shooter must be coming at full speed.

The second drill is the split-post drill. Now there are three men coming instead of two. They pass the ball back and forth, go past the postman, split and go for the layup. You can modify it and go for the jump shot, and you can also use a defensive postman.

The third drill is the three-lane rush drill on the full-court. We play full-court basketball, so why do we want to use half-court drills? You line three men up on the baseline, the three come down the floor in unison. The two wings are five feet ahead of the man in the middle. The ball progresses downcourt with no dribbles until you shoot the layup. This drill can also have one or two defensive players on each end of the court.

The fourth drill is the wide figure-eight. It makes for longer passes and longer routes to run. Everybody knows the figure-eight. The passer goes behind the man he passes to and you weave your way downcourt. Otherwise, it's the same as the third drill, the same three positions. In running this one, we do not let the wings come in closer than five feet from the sideline. We want them wide. We don't want a dribble unless the receiver is behind in floor position, and in that case, we allow one bounce. In this drill, the player never passes the ball behind his floor position. The player gets the layup, the wing opposite the shooter is the rebounder, he takes the ball out of the basket, the shooter swings under, goes out and now the person who passed to that shooter is naturally cutting behind him. The figure-eight begins again.

The fifth drill is our three-on-three full-court drill. If the player scores, he stops and takes the ball out, and the defense becomes the offense and vice versa. If the player misses, he uses the automatic pick-up rule. The player might be a guard having to defend a man 6'10" coming back. But we're playing basketball.

The sixth drill is our four-on-four drill, using a point guard, two wings and a postman. The offense makes a bucket, the defense takes the ball out and attacks. On a miss, of course, the defense attacks immediately. It's much more difficult to defend three-on-three or four-on-four than it is five-on-five. We call these last two our bread-and-butter drills.

The six drills encompass all skill executions except the free throw.

The only other drill we use is the basic body-position drill. A player assumes a defensive stance and slides his feet sideways, forwards, and backwards. It's a great drill for conditioning. If the player stays in a body-position drill for 20 minutes, then he can play 40 minutes without a gasp.

No longer do we say we're going to do five minutes of this and ten minutes of that. We do these by the numbers. For instance, we say we're going to shoot 25 on up to 35 or 40 in the layup drill. As a group, you have to make 25 or 35 in a row with the right hand, then come back and make that many with the left hand before you go to drill No. 2. The players don't advance to a new drill until they accomplish the goal. Same thing with the three-lane rush drill: If the goal is 15, that means 15 trips down and back. The players cannot miss a layup or drop the ball. If they do, you start over.

Some say you can't waste time. Well, we're not wasting time because the things we're doing are the basic requirements for basketball. The advantage of drills by the numbers is, first, it establishes who's boss—the coach is. Second, it makes the lowest man as important as the star. Third, the coach doesn't have to coach or reprimand individuals. You may be a freshman and not take me seriously, but upperclassmen will say, "Hey, junior, you want to do this all night?" If you don't do it right, we'll be doing it all day long and that's where we'll start tomorrow.

My juniors and seniors did the work for me. After a few weeks, we could accomplish all those drills in 15 minutes or less.

It has been said that drills are inherently boring. Some say you need to do a variety of things to keep players interested. Hogwash. The first cause of boredom is losing too many games. Second, it's drills without competition. Ask players what they enjoy most about practice, and they often say, "Scrimmaging."

Well, scrimmaging is a major part of this drill program.

And that's it. Those drills still work as beautifully today as they did earlier. We used them in our camps starting with youngsters at age 10. I've never seen drills better than these and I've kept my eye open a long time. Some say I'm old-fashioned because of it. But if it's not broken, don't fix it.

18

Reflections of a Retired Man

I've often been asked to come up with the superlatives in various categories in my career—best team, best player, etc. After 41 years in the business, it isn't always easy. I can say this without a moment's equivocation: There isn't any doubt about who my best point guard has been.

The Home Team

Over the years, Jean has been tremendously understanding of me and my professional travails. When you find a special woman like I did to stay with you for 47 years, you really have something extraordinary. I think it takes a very special kind of person to withstand the pressures a coach's wife has to go through. She has to be nice to fans and alumni when perhaps the first instinct might be to act otherwise.

Jean is intense about winning. As a matter of fact, she's more intense than I am about it. You have to give credit to wives married to coaches; they're going to suffer far more than the average wife. A coach lives each year running the gamut of emotions, and most of us become equipped to handle it pretty well. Fans can sometimes be harsh and it's the family that has to bear the brunt of it. The family has much to bear, sometimes far more than the coach himself.

It's tough, even on your children. I have a son, Paul, who is 6'3". So automatically, everybody thought he ought to be a basketball player. Well, he didn't want to be a basketball player at all, but just because he's the son of a coach, and he's 6'3", he should be a basketball player. Whoever thought that up?

One thing Jean will tell you is that I developed the knack of not bringing the game home with me. I guess I have a generally fatalistic attitude about life. You prepare as well as you can, do everything within your power to control things, but there are elements that simply can't be controlled. The ball that bounced directly to Pembrook Burrows to beat us in 1970 surely didn't have to go to him, but it did. No amount of anguishing or rehashing when I walked in the front door was going to change that. As I've said many times over the years, "That's the way the pickle squirts."

Jean suffered our games much harder than most. In the early years when our children were growing up, she wouldn't always attend. After the kids had grown up, she would go — until it got too tense, too noisy. Then she'd get up and walk out. She knows more about the campuses at Arizona and Arizona State, for instance, than I do. I think she could tell you more about the women's restrooms in all the arenas of the Pac-10 than any other person in America, including the maid that cleans them up.

> **Jean Miller: "If the truth were known, I don't think I was made to be a coach's wife. With Ralph, you'd never know it was the day of a game. He would sleep for at least two hours the afternoon of a game, and he was very matter-of-fact about it. I guess I can be grateful. I don't know if I could have put up with a person who was a pacer. We had a Big Ten game once that was very important, and I asked Ralph if he was dreading it like I was. He looked at me so strangely. He couldn't wait to get there. He always looked at a game as I do a game of bridge — the strategy involved, the joy in working against an opponent."**

We would always entertain in our hotel room after games on the road, but I suppose the circle of people I've shared our biggest moments with in basketball is relatively small. I do have close friends, but they usually have nothing to do with sports.

Fans

I've never wanted to be close to fans. Jean says I got it naturally from my father. If they want to talk basketball from a technical standpoint, I'll talk. I'm still not going to be buddy-buddy. It was the same way with my players. There's got to be a separation.

Some of that came from my father, but I think it also accrued from the giants of the game in the early days, Dr. Allen and Henry Iba. These kind of men had a stature that wasn't to be diminished by being a buddy. You're the head coach. The door is always open, but you can't always be a friend.

That's not to say I didn't develop awfully good friends through basketball. There were a couple of fellows I used to call my voluntary, elderly assistant coaches. Clifford Robinson — I always just called him Robby Robinson— would see the team off on every trip and would see them return. If it was one or two in the morning, Robby was there. For years and years, Robby rarely missed a practice.

Then there was Big Newt, Clarence Newton, an ex-FBI agent. He was a football player at Occidental and we met through a bridge group. He had never even been to a basketball game when we met, and all of a sudden, he became a big basketball fan. He took my basketball class three different times. On October 15, the opening day of practice for each season, these two would come up with something different. One time they dressed up in tuxedos and tennis shoes with orange bow ties, set up a card table with linen and had cookies and some cola from a champagne bottle. These are the people I call my real friends. I don't want to get too close to the average run-of-the-mill fan.

Small Pressures

The real pleasures in coaching are sometimes the small ones, subtle and insular. Certainly I've derived a great deal of satisfaction in winning, but you can't live only for that.

Bobby Cremins, the Georgia Tech coach, made an astute

observation at the Final Four in 1990. He said that he was once obsessed with making the Final Four, back in 1985 and 1986 when he was given a good shot at doing it. But in the intervening years, he had come to realize there was much more to what he was doing than merely participating in the Final Four. I certainly hope that's true.

One of the things I never managed to accomplish was playing in a Final Four, and that's a void that I wish I could have filled. Yet you grow to the conclusion that there is so much more to this profession. My initiation into the Hall of Fame was even more important to me than winning the national title. This represents longevity.

Maybe it's only the outgrowth of our tournament problems, but I don't think you should ever get wrapped up in one particular thing. It becomes overbearing. Once you get there, what are you going to do? You've got to play another game.

You'll never enjoy anything more than the pure pleasure of working with young people, and seeing not only what they accomplish as players but as people. They had a reunion at East High School a year or so ago, and a young man named Larry Jones was there, president of the board of the Coleman Company. Larry was the comptroller at one time at Wichita University — he used to sign my paychecks. A reporter asked him the question, did any of his teachers pass on anything he could remember that was important? He said, "No, not really, but my basketball coach, Ralph Miller, gave me a few things that have been very valuable to me throughout my life."

I had no idea. That came as a total shock to me. He was a graduate of Harvard Business School. I had no idea I could influence a kid with that kind of talent.

The Pro Game

I never had much desire to coach in the professional ranks. When I was 48 or 49 and in the latter part of my tenure at Iowa, I did get feelers from representatives of Chicago and Phoenix. Whether anyone was serious, I couldn't say.

My love of the game has always been centered on the high school and university level. I enjoyed working with younger people rather than established players who are already set in many ways. There is also an unwritten, but fundamental truth about pro basketball: Offense is the name of the game. It is spectator-oriented because of the need for revenue, so they set the stage by playing 48 minutes instead of 40, and with rules like the 24-second clock and the three-point shot. The rules emphasize offense, but today, defense is making a comeback and it shows in won-lost records.

I am, however, undefeated as a pro coach. My record is 1-0. In August of 1989, I was asked to coach a group of pros at a benefit game in Portland. Steve Johnson, who acted as my assistant coach, called me to give me a bad time about it.

"Did you really agree to coach a bunch of pros?" he asked.

"Well," I said, "let's define coaching. I wouldn't waste my time trying to tell any of you guys anything."

But Steve took the job seriously. He furnished complete capsules on all of the personnel — his twice as long as those of the other players. In fact, he made sure I knew he was grossly underpaid for his efforts. In reality, we shared equally; it was a benefit and nobody was paid.

We had fun with it. Before we went out for the game, I told my guys, "Listen, I have a reputation to uphold in the state of Oregon. Everyone knows I dislike the bounce pass. So we're only going to have this one rule: You can throw the bounce pass, but if it's dropped or muffed, whatever, we're calling a 20-second timeout, and I'm going to chew you out in public."

You know, we had a bunch of pros and in 48 minutes, we threw three bounce passes. Unfortunately, none of them went astray, and I never did get to call my 20-second timeout, but the thing that shocked me so much was, they listened.

Not that this endeared the bounce pass to me. I guess my dislike of it has become almost legendary. Basketball is only a matter of statistics, and I'll challenge anybody at any level of competition to count the turnovers and missed shot opportunities that occur from the bounce pass as opposed to the direct chest pass.

In the first place, when the ball hits the floor, the carom is never certain. It's especially hard for the big guys. Some of them adjust to it, but it's much more difficult to bend over and catch it at the knees than at the chest level. Most of the time, the passer can throw the ball directly to the receiver and not put it on the floor. For me, it's a question of time and space. You don't waste either one. You can't throw a bounce pass quicker than you can throw it through the air.

Problem is, I've had players who are pretty good at it. When I was a player, I could use the bounce pass. John Johnson could do it consistently. So could Gary Payton. But I was able to say, "Hey, Gary, they're going to drop too many of them."

If one guy can do it, then everybody on the team wants to try it.

I've had a lot of fun over the years with Tom Davis, a great exponent of the bounce pass. We're good friends, but I'll write him a note, saying, "Tom, I got to see your team play the other day and they weren't using the bounce pass. They looked much better. Congratulations."

Small Locales and Recruiting

In 38 years of coaching the college game, I was always in relatively small locales where the recruiting was harder and the road was difficult. Whether there is any deep psychology to that, I can't say.

Wichita was a medium-sized city, but we were clearly the third school in line in our state. Iowa and Oregon State each were in states that happened to be the smallest in population in both the Big Ten and Pac-10, respectively. The only factor I can relate to it, is that Jean and I both liked the college-town atmosphere rather than that of the big city. We liked the peace and quiet of the small community.

I remember Ray Meyer, the former DePaul coach, complaining back in the days of Mark Aguirre about the constant pressure of scouts and agents being around, interrupting practice, wanting to take the kids home. We never had that kind of foolishness in Corvallis.

I will say this. One of my mistakes in perception when I came to Oregon State was the hold UCLA had on recruiting—the total domination of John Wooden when he wanted a player. Anybody who came from another part of the country couldn't understand this, but it did exist. I don't think it was so much the proximity to Los Angeles for many players as it was simply the lure of

UCLA. When I was at Iowa, kids from Illinois, Ohio, and Indiana went everywhere. No one had a lock on those states. But certainly John really ruled the roost at UCLA.

We recruited a kid once who told me, "Coach, this is the only school I'm going to visit besides UCLA. To be honest, I just came up here to see if anything could be attractive to me."

When he left, I asked him, "Well, did you find anything of interest?"

"Nope," he said.

> **Dave Leach: "I think Ralph would have loved at one time to be coach at Kansas—between his Wichita State and Iowa days. When I was a junior and we tied for the Missouri Valley championship, we had a playoff game against Drake at KU. Somebody brought out a sign that said, 'Thanks Ralph, for bringing basketball back to KU.'**
>
> **"He compiled a record at some awfully tough places."**

Coaching Salaries and TV Money

There are some trends in the game that I can't say I like. This may be heresy, but coaching salaries have gone totally out of line, and I think they're part of the spiraling pressure to win. Now certainly coaching was good to me financially, although I didn't get independently rich. My salary at East High, combining teaching and coaching, was $3,200 a year. When I went to Wichita, it became $5,500. It certainly has changed. Even when I went to Oregon State in 1970, my salary, with no extras, came to $21,000.

Back about 1970, there were many conferences in the country that didn't think of basketball as a money-raising sport. The large arena came into being and soon after, you had the demand to support women's programs. If the coach didn't fill the arena, he was gone.

Now we have the other problems—what to do with the

television money, for example—and I'm not sure it's a good spiral at all. The motivation for coaching is to work with young people. I never suffered any less for a defeat in high school than I did in college. I think in terms of my heroes—the Ibas and Allens—and they coached for fun. Money had nothing to do with it. They didn't make that much.

In fact, I can remember a comment Dr. Allen made to me back when I was in college. We were talking about coaching and he said, "You know, the best jobs in America are the ones at the teachers colleges. You can make as much as I do at Kansas and the pressures are not nearly as great to win."

He put it in a nutshell. Everybody I've ever known who was an outstanding coach was an outstanding teacher. Not an outstanding recruiter or a super salesman, but a teacher.

Now we have this huge glut of money, mostly from television, as a result of the unprecedented popularity of college basketball. The latest CBS contract with the NCAA calls for one billion dollars over seven years. It's simply staggering, and it's a real irony that a fountain of largesse like this should be associated with so many of the problems in the game today.

Until recently, all we've done so far is add to the percentage for the competing teams, and I don't know if that's wise. I don't see how it follows the spirit of college athletics that we should simply award more money for the team that happens to win a game. That, too, is putting more pressure on coaches to get into the NCAA.

There are two better ways to handle the money. You could take the big pot, and divide it 293 ways for each school playing Division I basketball. The other route would be to include all Division I teams in the tournament, or make it a 256-team field, four times the size it is now. You could handle everybody in an extra week.

Cheating

I'm certainly of the opinion that cheating in college basketball has increased markedly in, say, the past 20 years. Much of it has to do with the increased pressure on the coach and the continuing money spiral.

John Thompson, the Georgetown coach, was quoted thusly: "Sometimes I wonder what dishonesty is. Is it dishonest to pay a kid . . . or is it just against the rules?"

Most people today agree that there is something wrong when athletes required to be pure amateurs can make millions for an athletic department, yet not be compensated. If a coach can conclude that that situation is immoral, it is then a short step to assure that recruits are paid.

In my coaching tenure, the most graphic example of cheating we came across involved one of my players, who happened to be over at a house visiting a player who eventually chose Oregon State. He sat and listened to an assistant coach offer a car to the recruit, and a washer and dryer to the mother.

Then we have the occasional charge of point-shaving, such as reared its head not long ago when a former North Carolina State player was alleged to have complied. Many fans today may not realize it, but that's a practice that was controversial more than 40 years ago, sweeping the country in infamous cases in New York City, at Kentucky, Bradley, and elsewhere.

Given the deprived economic status of many players today, and the money that could be gained from point-shaving, it is probably surprising it hasn't occurred more often. It's an easy way to turn a buck, and you're not asked to lose a game, just to keep it within range of a certain spread. At first look, that might not look bad to a player.

Back in the early 1950s, there was a rule adopted that you couldn't play a game off-campus. The idea was to shield players from the unfamiliar surroundings that might facilitate a point-shaving scam. I was back in New York City once in the 1950s for the East-West college all-star game, staying at the hotel where they were keeping the respective teams. I saw one of the players and said, "Hi, how are you, hope you have a good game." Suddenly, there was a detective on my shoulder. He wanted to know what I was doing talking to this kid. The tournament hosts had hired detectives to police the halls and ensure that no gamblers talked to players.

On another occasion in the 1950s when I was at Wichita, I got a call from the president of the school, Dr. Harry Corbin, who had been informed by friends that there had been a drastic swing in the point spread on our game that night with Western Kentucky. He simply wanted me to be aware of it in case there would be any situation that could in any way be deemed questionable.

I made it a general habit to try to know what the odds were. I suppose there was a feeling that it was better, if possible, to stay away from the borderline, point-spread situation where a play or a coaching move might be questioned. Most coaches were aware of the odds. People in that time period were very conscious of the gambling element because of the widespread scandal.

If cheating is up and every school around is recruiting blacks, is it harder to find the "sleepers" that made our program thrive for so long? Even in the latter part of the Wichita days, the Texas schools were not using blacks, so that was kind of open territory; it created a wider pool of opportunity. Yet sleepers are still out there. Sometimes the only difference between a blue-chip high school recruit and a great player in college is that one developed earlier than the other.

Remember, Lester Conner didn't even make his starting five in high school. A.C. Green probably should have been a blue-chipper; he bloomed relatively late. Gary Payton was more heavily recruited, but not as heavily as his stock of today would reflect. So they're out there. They may not be hidden as thoroughly as Steve Johnson was, but they're out there.

Best Players, Teams, and Victories

At the risk of offending some friends, then, let's have a little fun and put together some superlative players, teams, and moments I've seen over 41 years.

The five best college basketball teams I've ever seen:

1.   UCLA, 1969. It had not only Lew Alcindor as a senior—the pre-eminent big man of the era—but the sophomore forwards, Curtis Rowe and Sidney Wicks. UCLA won the national championship by 20 points over Purdue, marking the first time in history any school had won three consecutive national titles. The final game marked the end of Alcindor's three-year, 88-2 reign over college basketball.

2. Kansas, 1952. This was the introduction of half-court pressure defense—an offshoot of Gene Johnson's 2-2-1—plus the dominance of Clyde Lovellette. He scored basically 30 points a game, one of the great scorers. In its last three games in the NCAA tournament that year, this team won by 19, 19, and 17.

3. San Francisco, 1956. This was a startling team. You hadn't seen any postman who could play defense like Bill Russell. They also had K.C. Jones. A very solid basketball team.

4. UCLA, 1973. The junior year of the Walton Gang. Walton's final calling-card that year was a 21-for-22 shooting night against Memphis State.

5. Cincinnati, 1962. It was a shocker when Cincy beat Ohio State in overtime for the 1961 title. They did it again to the same team in 1962, convincingly, 71-59.

The five best collegiate players:

Postman—**Lew Alcindor, UCLA**. The best all-around center.

Forward—**Elvin Hayes, Houston**. Only question would be his defense, but just a heck of a good player.

Forward—**Michael Jordan, North Carolina**. Forward here rather than guard. Became a pro unequaled, but wasn't bad in college, either.

Guard—**Magic Johnson, Michigan State**. At 6' 9", heralded a new era in size on the perimeter.

Guard—**Oscar Robertson, Cincinnati**. Might have been better all-around than Magic. There wasn't anything he couldn't do. Robertson wasn't noted for his defense, but when he wanted to play it, he could.

The five best college coaches:

1. John Wooden, UCLA.
2. Phog Allen, Kansas.
3. Henry Iba, Oklahoma State.
4. Ray Meyer, DePaul.
5. Adolph Rupp, Kentucky.

The five toughest arenas:

1.   Pauley Pavilion, UCLA, 1971-1989. Much of it had to do with those banners. When we finally won there in late February, 1981, we were still undefeated and other people were having success at UCLA, but it was still a huge victory for us.

2.   Robertson Fieldhouse, Bradley, 1952-1964.   Thirteen times we went there, 13 times we lost.

3.   Armory Field House, University of Cincinnati, 1958-1964. Cincy was the dominant team of that era.

4.   Gallagher Hall, Oklahoma State, 1952-1964. Blood Alley, it was called. Iba's defense, protecting the middle, and the atmosphere made it a miserable place to play.

5.   McArthur Court, Oregon, 1971-1977. For my friends in Eugene. It wasn't so much the scoreboard bouncing above the court, it was the fans lining the floor on four sides.

The five coaches I most enjoyed beating:

1. John Wooden, UCLA.
2. Henry Iba, Oklahoma State.
3. Eddie Hickey, St. Louis.
4. Dick Harter, Oregon.
5. John Ravenscroft, Newton, Kansas High School.

The five best teams I coached:

1. Iowa, 1970 and Oregon State, 1981. You'll never get me to break that tie. But the Iowa group was probably the best all-around team I ever had.

3. Oregon State, 1980. A younger version of OSU 1981, but without Lester Conner.

4. Oregon State, 1982. Went to the NCAA final eight and had amazing cohesiveness.

5. Wichita State, 1964. Stallworth and Bowman, for starters.

My five most satisfying victories in coaching:

1. Wichita East High School 62, Newton 48 at Emporia, Kansas, 1951. Our state AA championship.

2. Wichita University 67, Oklahoma A&M 66, at Stillwater, Oklahoma, 1954. First win ever for Wichita over Henry Iba's team on the road.

3. Wichita State 59, Cincinnati 58, at Cincinnati, 1964. First-ever win for Shockers at Cincy.

4. Oregon State 82, UCLA 76, at Los Angeles, 1981. First win ever for OSU at Pauley Pavilion, and it sustained a 25-game winning streak.

5. Iowa 87, UCLA 82, at Chicago, 1965. My first Iowa team against that year's national champions.

The five best offensive players I have coached:

Center—Steve Johnson, Oregon State.
Forward—Dave Stallworth, Wichita State.
Forward—John Johnson, Iowa.
Guard—Fred Brown, Iowa.
Guard—Gary Payton, Oregon State (he wasn't a bad defender, either).

The five best defensive players I have coached:

Center—Gene Wiley, Wichita State.
Forward—Lonnie Shelton, Oregon State.
Forward—A.C. Green, Oregon State.
Guard—Freddie Boyd, Oregon State.
Guard—Lester Conner, Oregon State.

The five best shooters I have coached:

1.   Dave Stallworth. Could shoot from anywhere. Probably the most complete of all the players I had.

2.   Steve Johnson. No great range, but it's hard to overlook a .746 season like he had in 1981.

3.   Fred Brown. And he might have been a better passer than he was a shooter.

4.   Rocky Smith, Oregon State. One of the few guys I thought should have made the pros and didn't. As pure a shooter from outside as anybody I've had.

5.   John Johnson. Still holds the Iowa record for field goals in a season at 289.

19

The Best of Both Worlds

So how is retirement treating me? In a word, wonderfully. It's a great lifestyle.

The nicest thing about retirement is that you don't have to make any plans. Time is not important. I don't have to leave the house at 6:00 a.m. to catch a flight to see a recruit in Los Angeles. I don't have to be out at practice at 2:00 p.m. I don't have to wait for the manager's word on when there are six minutes left before tip-off.

I'm glad to get rid of this telephone. I've spent a good many hours on it over the years and it takes a toll. Who knows how many conversations I've had with recruits, supervisors of officials, sportswriters?

My hearing has slacked off somewhat in recent years, but overall, my health has been good. Granted, there are those who think I'd be better off without a pack of cigarettes in my pocket.

I've smoked since I was in college. Now it seems to be something that almost precedes me. In almost every reference to me the subject of smoking is mentioned. It's just like when George Raveling told the joke about me being the origin of the whiskey sour drink. That one has been retold so many times it just seems to be part of my baggage.

Lanny Van Eman: "In the bigger cities, we used to take taxicabs to and from the game. After one game in St. Louis when I was playing, Ron

Heller and I were sitting in the back seat of a cab and Ralph was in front. He fumbled for his cigarettes; he couldn't find them.

"Well, Ron smoked. At that time, smoking and drinking by players was strictly taboo, but Ron smoked. I knew he did, and other players knew it. Anyway, Ralph found some matches, turned around and said, 'Ron, give me a cigarette.' Ron was somewhat stunned. He looked at me, like, 'Should I or shouldn't I?' But he fumbled it up to Ralph, and Ralph proceeded to commiserate on the game."

I doubt if I've been interviewed very many times when the subject of smoking did not come up. Then I became a *chain smoker* in news stories. It's like the adjective "crochety." I haven't seen very many write-ups on me in recent years that didn't use the term crochety. I'm not sure I even know what that word means.

With smoking, at least I didn't come off as a hypocrite. I smoked around my teams. So they knew it. I never wanted to be hypocritical. I smoke, so I smoke, and you ought to know it. It was written that in the later years, I'd often watch practice in a chair next to the court, cigarette and ashtray at my side. Well, that was true. But I wasn't hiding anything.

Yes, there are other stories about me and my cigarettes. At an Iowa team banquet one year, one of our guys got up and told about an occasion in the locker room at halftime when I was just getting down to brass tacks on a subject, pulled a cigarette from the pack and lit it—the filter, that is.

After I finally retired, Fifi Anderson, Jim Anderson's wife, decided it would be nice if the new head coach began his career at Oregon State in a freshly cleansed office. Rumor has it there was a film of considerable thickness on the walls.

One of our former part-time assistants used to say that Ralph Drollinger, the former UCLA center who was into nature trails and mountain climbing, was so taken aback by my smoking that he ruled out Oregon State. But that's me. What you see is what you get.

Another story that has made the rounds is that when we were in the home of Stuart Gray—the center who later attended UCLA—in southern California, I mistook a wooden coaster for an ashtray and deposited some ashes in it, raising eyebrows. You can't prove it by me.

Jimmy Anderson used to say that the briefcase I carried on road trips had only cartons of cigarettes in it. He claimed it had nothing to do with important papers.

Jean Miller: "I don't remember Ralph not smoking. He's always smoked. Oh, there was a period when he'd stop for awhile, but it's been a part of him all these years.

"That is the one thing he's very sensitive about. His doctor has had a fit about it for years."

I had my physical exam just recently, they took my EKG and the nurse's aide ran it down to the doctor. She came back and said, "Everything's fine, but the doctor told me to tell you to quit smoking." I said, "What's new, he's been telling me that for 15 years."

When I came to Oregon State in 1970, I had quit for five or six months, but I really didn't try very hard and started up again. Does Jean get after me about it? Daily.

One publicized malady I've had on a rare occasion is Meniere's disease. It's an inner-ear disorder in which an excess of lymphatic fluid presses on the labyrinth. The usual symptoms are dizziness, chills, and sometimes vomiting. In some instances, progressive attacks over the years can result in severe deafness.

It happened to me first when I was 27 years old though it was not diagnosed at that time. My case was not actually diagnosed until I was about 50. My attacks were always minor. They always seem to start with a chill. I shudder a couple of times and then it's time to go home, get into bed, pull up the covers and go to sleep. If I can do that for a couple of hours, I'll wake up and be fine.

I haven't suffered as severely as some people have. I feel for the people who get the disease. I have a nephew who is afflicted with it all the time. On occasion, he'll have to be in bed for a week.

I had a severe attack of Meniere's in my last year at Iowa, and my last one was after a trip we took at Oregon State to play Utah. I took a shower at 8:00 a.m., got dressed, and began getting the chills. Then I went to the airport with a guy who seemed as if he was trying to qualify for the Indianapolis 500. By the time I got to the airport, I had all the symptoms — chilling, a terrible headache, and nausea. So they put me in a wheelchair and in the meantime, Jimmy called my wife. She came to the airport in Eugene and announced that we were going directly to the doctor's office to check me out. I pleaded my case, telling her I knew full well what it was. I just wanted to go home and get in bed.

Well, we sat around the doctor's office for an hour or so and they sent me home. After I stayed in bed for a couple of hours, I was fine.

My final season at OSU produced a good deal of nostalgia, as well as some astonishing kindness by the schools that hosted us.

Stanford presented me a new golf bag; the Far West Classic people gave me a set of gold-plated Pings. Arizona State provided air fare, lodging, and golf in Tempe. George Raveling at USC did the same for a trip to San Diego. Washington State donated airfare and lodging at Lake Coeur d'Alene, and the Harshmans at Washington presented us with tickets for a Caribbean cruise. Oregon gave Jean and me matching rocking chairs. Arizona even kicked in assorted bottles of scotch, gladly accepted.

Then in September, 1989, the people at Oregon State gave me a wonderful send-off. Mike Corwin, the sports information director for basketball, did a major share of the organization, and they brought back a good many of the coaches and players I had with me over the years for a banquet and program. It was done in a surprise, *This-Is-Your-Life* type of format. It was a night to remember. They added a brand new four-wheel drive vehicle for the snowy roads around our home at Black Butte, and announced the renaming of Ralph Miller Drive adjacent to Gill Coliseum.

Since I turned the reins over to Jimmy in the spring of 1989, my wife and I have been on the go so much, it sometimes doesn't seem as though the pace has eased all that drastically.

Jean and I have spent time traveling to southern California to visit her family. In January of 1990, we went back to Chanute. When I was a junior in high school, the gymnasium, which was about six or seven years old then, burned down. It was re-vamped, and then the board of education decided to build a new one across the street on which I lived once, Evergreen. They were nice enough to name the new gym after me and it was dedicated in January.

No, Chanute hasn't changed much. It never really changed. It's much like the average Midwestern town, the people don't change much. The hotel's closed now. There are no shopping malls. A home-town boy can still find the house in which he was born, or lived in all his life. I lived in six different houses and they're all there. Most of them haven't even been painted.

The railroad still goes through there, but it's dead compared to what it used to be. The diesel engine put division headquarters like Chanute out of business. The roundhouse disappeared. After World War II, the engine was hooked on in Kansas City and the train went on to Tulsa with no problem.

Even in retirement, there's always something coming up. I attended a couple of Oregon State basketball games last winter, but you won't see me much around Gill Coliseum. I don't covet the attention given to those occasions, and I certainly don't want to be peering over Jimmy's shoulder.

As for other activities, we had a family reunion scheduled for late summer, 1990, at Black Butte. I've got a Nike function to attend. And the 1970 Iowa team had a 20-year reunion recently in Iowa City.

For the first time in 20 years, I don't have a Corvallis address anymore. We sold our house there in the spring of 1990, and now call two different spots home. One is in the mountains at Black Butte Ranch, in a house we've had for several years designed by my son Paul. The other is a place on the coast at Newport. There aren't very many more beautiful places in the world than Black Butte, and you could say the same about Newport. If it snows too much up in the mountains, I can always come down to the seashore. We've got the best of both worlds.

Jean says I'm "domestic" and if that means I would rather do housework than gardening, she is right. I've always pitched in with the work around the home—including changing diapers— so you might say, I was a house husband before it was "cool."

I've become quite a house painter. Jean thinks I'm kind of a fanatic about it. But I'd rather get it done today because if I don't, I've got to do it tomorrow. And there are too many other better things to do tomorrow.

Although I have referred to various members of our family throughout, Jean and I had two sets of children, Susan and Cappy, then Paul and Shannon. There are 15 years between our daughters, and I highly recommend this procedure. We have enjoyed the longevity of parenthood. To our great sorrow, Cappy died from apnea, a little known problem then, but one that is being highly researched now. We have seven grandchildren at present and Shannon will provide us with the eighth soon.

I find it very relaxing and nice to be at this stage of my life. No regrets whatsoever. I'm not one of those people who has difficulty switching off the clock. In fact, I rarely find myself putting on a watch. There's got to be a specific reason to have one on.

I want my peace and quiet. I suppose that's part of where my nap custom originated. I never have minded being alone. I don't have to have company. I enjoy it, but I don't have to have it. I like traveling, but I like to stay at home, too. I like the solitude. Maybe that's why I live in the mountains. I think there are times when everybody should be to themselves.

I had a wonderful time as a coach, but now coaching has passed. Great, let's go on to something new. Now I can sit and watch a game and feel sorry for those poor suckers out there on the bench, trying to win a silly ball game.

I've made a pledge to myself, to get back on that golf course more often. I haven't even had enough time for that, and my handicap is up there right now — at 19 — where I know I can make money. I'll have to admit, though, there are days on the golf course that I swear I'm going to take up lawn bowling instead.

How do I want to be remembered? If they want to put something like this on my tombstone, that's all right: "He wasn't a bad teacher."